Q.B.L.

Q.B.L.

or
The Bride's Reception

Being a Qabalistic Treatise
on the Nature and Use
of the Tree of Life

Frater Achad
Introduction by Lon Milo DuQuette

WEISER BOOKS
Boston, MA/York Beach, ME

This edition first published in 2005 by

Red Wheel/Weiser, LLC
York Beach, ME
With offices at:
368 Congress Street
Boston, MA 02210
www.redwheelweiser.com

The Library of Congress has cataloged the original hardcover edition as follows: 70-16454

ISBN 1-57863-331-1

Typeset in the United States
Printed in Canada
TCP

12 11 10 09 08 07 06 05

8 7 6 5 4 3 2 1

The paper used in this publication meets the minimum requirements of the American National Standard for Information Sciences—Permanence of Paper for Printed Library Materials Z39.48-1992 (R1997).

אחד

אהבה

CONTENTS

INTRODUCTION TO THE
2005 EDITION

I, _____ a member of the Body of God, hereby
bind myself on behalf of the Whole Universe, even as I
am now physically bound unto the cross of suffering,
that I will lead a spiritual life, as a devoted servant of the
Order; that I will love all things; that I will experience
all things and endure all things; that I will continue in
the Knowledge and Conversation of my Holy Guardian
Angel; that I will work without attachment; that I will
work in truth; that I will rely ultimately upon myself;
that I shall realize my True Will; that I will interpret
every phenomenon as a particular dealing of God with
my Soul.[1]

And if I fail therein, may my pyramid be profaned, and
the Eye closed to me.

As I wrote in the preface to W. H. Müller's *Polaria. The
Gift of the White Stone*:

The above declaration is known as the "Oath of the Abyss." Whosoever utters it with full magical intention invokes a terrible curse upon themselves, for they are either hopelessly deluded and committing an act of supreme spiritual presumption, or they have balanced and perfected all aspects of what most of us consider to be the "self" and are now prepared to take the last irrevocable step toward becoming more than human. In both cases, the world will presume they have gone mad.[2]

On the summer solstice of 1916 Charles Robert John Stansfeld Jones (Frater Achad),[3] an accountant from Vancouver and an $A\therefore A\therefore$ Neophyte $(1° = 10^{\square})$,[4] formally took the Oath of the Abyss, thereby laying claim (in accordance with the traditions of that august fraternity) to the initiatory title, Master of the Temple $(8° = 3^{\square})$.

Jones dutifully reported this event in a telegram to Aleister Crowley, his superior in the Order, who nine months earlier in September had labored in vain (he thought) to beget a child with his "scarlet woman," Jeanne Robert Foster.[5] Crowley was amazed by circumstances of Jones's initiation and the timing of the event. He wrote in his *Confessions*:

> Every cause must produce its proper effect; so that, in this case, the son whom I willed to beget came to birth on a plane other than the material. . . . What I had really done was therefore to beget a Magical Son. So, precisely nine months afterwards, that is at the summer solstice of 1916, Frater O.I.V. (the Motto of C. Stansfeld Jones as a

Probationer) entirely without my knowledge became a Babe of the Abyss.[6]

Jones's apparant success also represented in Crowley's mind a stunning validation of the A∴A∴ system of magical attainment. The proud "father" gushed:

> I could only conclude that his success was almost
> wholly due to the excellence of the system which I had
> given to the world. In short, it was the justification of
> my whole life, the unique and supreme reward of my
> immeasurable toils.[7]

Crowley's confidence in Achad was further bolstered by a string of "discoveries" Jones would soon make—vital Qabalistic keys that unlocked fundamental mysteries of *The Book of the Law*[8] and the Aeon of Horus. Some of these were outlined in a short, posthumously published book, *Liber 31*,[9] which Jones sent Crowley in 1919. Crowley couldn't have been happier with the revelations: "Your key opens the Palace."[10]

It seemed in Achad, Crowley truly had found "the one" foretold in *The Book of the Law*: "... the one to follow thee,"[11] the one "... who shall discover the Key of it all"[12]—the magical child and brilliant heir apparent to the Great Beast and Prophet of the Aeon of Horus.

Perhaps he had. But the father-son relationship these two great adepts shared would not endure to the end. Eventually it would become strained to the breaking point, and amazingly, we know the exact day this beautiful relationship began

to sour. We have a written record of the precise moment—
the moment Frater Achad either experienced a quantum
leap in consciousness or stepped off the zenith edge of supernal adeptship into the abyss of occult madness.[13]

It happened on May 31, 1922, as Jones was writing the
fourth chapter of *Q. B. L. or The Bride's Reception*—a moment
that would literally turn the Qabalistic universe upside down.

> I had written thus far (May 31st, 1922 E.V.) when I was
> rewarded with the opening up of SECRETS so won-
> derful that they have changed my whole conception of
> the Plan of the Qabalah, and have indeed proved not
> alone a LIGHTNING FLASH to destroy THE
> HOUSE OF GOD but a SERPENT of WISDOM to
> re-construct it, and yet again a STAR which explains all
> SYMBOLISM. This matter being of such TRAN-
> SCENDENT IMPORTANCE will be dealt with in
> the form of Appendixes to this Volume which will be
> obtainable under certain special conditions. Meanwhile
> the main plan of this book will be followed as origi-
> nally intended, since it is necessary that the Student
> should have a clear and comprehensive grasp of the old
> system before he could appreciate the New.[14]

Fortunately for us, Jones did indeed follow the original
plan of the text through to completion and saved elucida-
tions on his revolutionary theories for the book's appendixes. This thoughtful gesture, in my opinion, renders the
main text of *Q.B.L.* the clearest, most understandable, and
practical introduction to the study of Qabalah written to

that date. It also effectively prepares the more Qabalistically educated reader for the provocative ideas presented in the appendixes—concepts that suggest that the traditional allocation of the letters of the Hebrew alphabet upon the 22 Paths of the Tree of Life should be in essence *reversed* in their positions.

Such a suggestion isn't necessarily heretical, especially when posited from the point of view of a Master of the Temple ($8° = 3^{\square}$), an adept whose consciousness abides above the Abyss that separates the Supernal Triad of the Tree of Life (Kether-Chokmah-Binah)—an Abyss below which *division is the result of contradiction*, and above which *contradiction is unity*.

Crowley, however, was not impressed with what he considered to be Achad's flawed and immature grasp of this "rule of contraries." He would later write:

> But this rule must be applied with skill and discretion, if error is to be avoided. It is a lamentable fact that worthy Zelator of A∴A∴, one Frater Achad, having been taught (patiently enough) by the Seer to use this formula, was lured by his vanity to suppose that he had discovered it himself, and proceeded to apply it indiscriminately. He tried to stand the Serpent of Wisdom on its head, and argued that as he was a ($1° = 10^{\square}$) of the Order, he must equally be a ($10° = 1^{\square}$)! As *The Book of Lies* says, "I wrenched DOG backwards to find God; now God barks!" He would have been better advised to reverse his adored ONE and taken a dose of ENO!"[15]

A year later, in 1923, upon receipt of Achad's next book, *The Egyptian Revival*, Crowey voiced in his diary his exasperation with the direction his "son" was taking.

What line shall I take with regard to Frater Achad's books? (I have just received The Egyptian Revival & a threat of others.) The point is this—the books—even apart from the absurd new attribution proposed for the Paths—are so hopelessly bad in almost every way— English, style, sense, point of view, oh everything!—yet they may do good to people they are written for. My real concern is lest he get too much ubris [hubris] and come a real cropper.[16]

His fears become (at least in Crowley's mind) a reality. He wrote in *Magick in Theory and Practice*:

One who ought to have known better tried to improve the Tree of Life by turning the Serpent of Wisdom upside down! Yet he could not even make his scheme symmetrical: his little remaining good sense revolted at the supreme atrocities. Yet he succeeded in reducing the whole Magical Alphabet to nonsense, and shewing that he had never understood its real meaning.

The absurdity of any such disturbance of the arrangement of the Paths is evident to any sober student from such examples as the following. Binah, the Supernal Understanding, is connected with Tiphereth, the Human Consciousness, by Zain, Gemini, the Oracles of the Gods, or the Intuition. That is, the attribution represents a psychological fact: to replace it by The Devil is either humour or plain idiocy. Again, the card "Fortitude," Leo, balances Majesty and Mercy with Strength and Severity: what sense is there in putting "Death," the Scorpion, in its stead? There are twenty other mistakes in the new wonderful illuminated-from-on-high attribution; the student can therefore be sure of twenty more laughs if he cares to study it.[17]

Tell us how you really feel, Mr. Crowley!

Of course it can be argued that Crowley was simply jealous of Achad's discoveries, the speed of his initiatory advancement, and his independent spirit. After all, Crowley could be viciously cruel and petty. It must be pointed out, however, that no matter how bitterly he railed against Jones's new doctrines he always acknowledged and praised his role as the discoverer of the Qabalistic key to *Liber AL vel Legis*, or *The Book of the Law*.

The fact remains that Jones's behavior as the years progressed led many to believe that he suffered bouts of mental illness. Such things are hard to prove, especially where magicians are concerned, and should not necessarily cast negative aspersions upon the quality of his work done during healthier times, or negate the real possibility such behavior manifested because Jones was enraptured in inscrutably high levels of consciousness.

He would join the Roman Catholic Church in an attempt to transmute this world religion into one that accepts the Law of Thelema and the formula of the Age of Horus.

But was that an act of insanity or simply the bold and auda-
cious act of a Thelemic hero? Yes, he would be put away for
flinging aside his raincoat to expose his nakedness to the
masses of Vancouver. But are the naked Sadhus of India
imprisoned for indecency?

It is easy for us (especially those of us whose initiatory
careers place us conspicuously low on the Tree of Life) to
point to these incidents and speculate how Achad's prema-
ture advance to Master of the Temple caused his ultimate fall
into the madness of Daäth (the false Sephira, "Knowledge,"
that resides in the Abyss itself) to become a Black Brother. In
truth, very few people on the face of the earth are qualified
to make that judgment. Certainly not I.

Achad himself, however, gives us a chilling hint of his
thoughts on this matter in a 1948 letter to Gerald Yorke:

> If this New Æon is what it seems to be, it will have
> lifted the Curse of the Magus and destroyed the
> Glamour and Lies and Madness of the Supernal Paths.
> That would leave one in Daäth—and represent real
> Attainment—the becoming one with Those Who
> Know.[18]

Speculation and controversy aside, Frater Achad remains
one of the most interesting and important magical figures
of the 20th century. His initial Qabalistic discoveries continue to yield new and provocative ideas concerning *The
Book of the Law* and other Holy Books of Thelema.

Q. B. L. or *The Bride's Reception* is a masterpiece of Qabalah
and controversy. Its importance to the world of modern

occult literature can be measured not only by its value as a remarkably understandable textbook of the fundamental principles of Qabalah, but also by the way it offers us a rare glimpse into the heart and mind of a brilliant and sincere seeker of wisdom and truth.

LON MILO DUQUETTE, COSTA MESA, CALIFORNIA

Editor's note:

The first and subsequent editions of *Q.B.L. or The Bride's Reception* retained the author's curious and inconsistent capitalization, bolding, and underlining of certain words and phrases. While it is obvious in many cases that these irregularities were simply done to indicate italics or other typographical enhancements not executable on a manual typewriter, there are also instances where the author might have been trying to communicate something of a more esoteric nature. After much discussion, the editors of this new edition resolved not to engage in guesswork and risk undermining what might have been the author's intent or emphasis. Therefore, with the exception of editor's footnotes and corrections made from the original errata sheet, the text remains a faithful reproduction of the original.

INTRODUCTION

Philosophically speaking, a great deal of rubbish has accumulated around the roots of The Tree of Life, and this has certainly deterred some truly hungry and thirsty souls from participation in the fruitful feast that awaits all who have the courage, patience, and it may be, daring to claim their Divine Inheritance.

This Inheritance, many have been content to exchange for a Mess of Pottage. In fact, even prior to the time of Esau and Jacob, ever since our forefather Adam was persuaded to accept a sour and half-chewed apple as the Whole Fruit, his descendents have suffered, very much as the small schoolboy suffers, crying "Never again, I'm through with forbidden fruit forever."

If one were to be swayed by the learned but destructive criticism of Mr. Ginsburg,[1] sickened by the puerilities of some Mystics who ought to know better, deceived by the apparent grossness of the Secret Schools, whose exponents do know better, to say nothing of becoming poisoned by the unwarranted efforts of deliberate deceivers and their ignorant dupes, one might well follow the example of the small school-boy and leave the fruit of the Qabalistic Tree alone.

But, fortunately, there is an aspect of this Work, slightly different from those usually considered, which is—or has been to me—of great interest and importance.

Let me first give due credit and thanks to all those who in the Past and in the Present have transmitted the fragments of the Secret Wisdom and have done so much towards fashioning them into a complete System of Attainment, the fruit of whose labours I have unhesitatingly used, as all True Initiates intend their followers should do. That I do not mention These by Name, is not through lack of courtesy, but rather that I feel it desirable to confuse the issue as little as possible. In other words, although the Holy Qabalah must, of course, have a History, just for once, I intend to take the liberty of leaving aside the Historical Background, and with it the squabbles over its Origin, as to whether it was In the Beginning transmitted by God to the Angels and in turn to Men or whether it arose from obscurity within the last 1800 years, considering rather its PRESENT USE.

We should learn to take advantage of the Past, using the scaffolding of the Temple and such ideas connected therewith as are of use in our particular case, adding thereto the results of our own investigations. In other words, we shall find in the "Tree of Life" and its correspondences A CONVENIENT MEANS OF CLASSIFICATION, a sort of Filing Cabinet, together with much valuable material ready to file, and room for all that we may collect in our future researches.

We shall find in this "Filing Cabinet" a means of GET-TING RID of a great many IDEAS which have been valueless on account of their unbalanced nature, and this, not by means of suppression—which forms complexes—but by careful arrangement, thus setting our minds in Order and by Balancing these ideas against their Opposites, leaving the Mind in a state which transcends both aspects, thus gradually regaining our lost EQUILIBRIUM which is the BASIS of the WORK.

The intention of this essay is to supply a basis whereby all serious Students of the Occult and Mystic Lore may learn to attain to Equilibrium on all Planes, thus gradually taking up their Great Inheritance, and while climbing higher and higher towards the Summit of the Work, planting their feet yet more firmly upon a sure foundation, that of **Direct Experience**. To such as succeed in their endeavours, history will matter little, except in-so-far as it represents their own early struggles or it may be gives hints of the means to be employed, but in the End, they will find themselves at One with the Beginning, citizens of that Kingdom wherein all is HERE and NOW.

CHAPTER ONE

The Formation of the Tree of Life Being "A Qabalistic Conception of the Creative Process"

It may be well to warn the casual reader of this treatise that its Title "THE BRIDE'S RECEPTION" is not intended to imply that the contents will read exactly like a French Novel. I shall make no attempt to explain my choice of this title, but rather rely upon it attracting those who have already made at least a superficial study of the Holy Qabalah, sufficient to enable them to get a glimpse of its meaning.

On the other hand, let not those who are serious in their search for more Light rashly turn aside on account of the initial difficulty of what may seem to them a New System, or a different presentation of an Old One.

It is essential to my present purpose that some outline be given of the Formation of the Tree of Life and this not alone in graphic form, although the graphic presentation is very important, forming a clear-cut conception of our "Filing Cabinet" which must be strongly impressed upon our minds in order that we may mentally refer to it at a moment's notice. The development of the ideas involved naturally comes first, however, so that I must ask my readers to lay aside previous

conceptions and give me their complete and careful attention, to which should be added repeated study if necessary,
until they are in a position to grasp what undoubtedly is an
abstruse subject for the beginner.

The word "QABALAH" is derived from the Hebrew
Root קבל—QBL, meaning "TO RECEIVE," and from this
source we may indeed RECEIVE of the Fruit of the "Tree
of Life." We must first, however, learn to transcend the
"KNOWLEDGE of GOOD and EVIL" and, in fact, all the
so-called "Pairs of Opposites," for it is written "EQUILIB-
RIUM IS THE BASIS OF THE WORK."[1]

The study of the Holy Qabalah will help us to attain this
Equilibrium, but we should give heed to the hidden warn-
ing implied by TAROT in the very Root (QBL) itself, "The
Illusion of the **Juggler** with the **Balance**."[2]

In the Beginning, the Qabalists tell us, there was NOTH-
ING—אין—AIN. I must refer my readers to the Essay enti-
tled BERASHITH[3] should they wish to enquire further in
regard to the Absoluteness of the Qabalistic Zero, and I may
add their study will be well repaid.

This AIN is a conception entirely beyond the possibilities of human thought, it being, so to speak, the absence of
all known qualities including the idea of "zero" itself.

There is another "veil of the negative" which the Qabalists
call AIN SUPH (אין סוף)—WITHOUT LIMIT. This is
referred to Infinite Space, the Infinitely Great as AIN may
be considered the Infinitely Small,[4] yet SPACE bereft of any
known qualities and therefore impossible of conception by
the finite mind.

Once again they added a "veil" to the Primal Nothingness of the Beginning, AUR (אוֹר) LIGHT, thus obtaining AIN SUPH AUR, the Limitless Light of Chaos.

Even here the mind falls back unable to grasp what is still a negative conception until we consider this Boundless Light of Infinity as CONCENTRATING in upon ITSELF to a CENTRE, or POINT of Focus, and this we may apprehend only in-so-far as we too have succeeded in focusing our Light in the Centre of our own Being, thus obtaining, when all else disappears, a Consciousness of the Great Unity of All Things, the SELF-EXISTENT CROWN of BEING.

This CROWN the Qahalists designate KETHER and symbolize by the POINT within the CIRCLE, attributing to It the NUMBER ONE, the basis of all Numbers, indivisible, capable by multiplication of producing nothing but Itself, incapable of addition to Itself save by REFLEXION in the Nothingness from whence it arose.

We can none of us doubt the fact of our own EXISTENCE, or at least of the Existence of SOMETHING, call it CONSCIOUSNESS or what we will. The WHY of this existence we know not and indeed the fact that It is UNKNOWN insures It as BEING beyond the possibility of DOUBT. The Realization of this Existence is not obtained by inference or deduction or by any Known process; It is beyond and above Knowledge and to doubt It but implies the Existence of One who doubts or denies.

Should such a One be capable of blotting out from consciousness every known quality of the Universe, and of Self, including the Wisdom which makes the manifestation of these Qualities possible, yet that One could only say "There remains SOMETHING which EXISTS and which COMPREHENDS NOTHING." Should He again seek to **comprehend** that SOMETHING, he must turn back again upon Himself, creating thereby a certain SEEMING DUALITY in order that the Self may thus comprehend Itself. Thus also the ONE by focusing Itself Within, first comprehendeth ITS essential Qualities, which may then be said to become Manifest.

Firstly cometh the idea of WISDOM, which the Qabalists call CHOKMAH, and with it the Great Illusion of Maya, "I am I," or SELF-RECOGNITION. But with this conception is brought to birth its eternal mate UNDERSTANDING—BINAH—and through this doth the ONE Understand that "This that is perceived" is "NOT—I," thus denying the Existence of the Phenomenal Self as being other than the REFLEXION of Truth, and herein lieth the Root of Sorrow, even as in Chokmah lieth the Root of Change.

In order to make this most difficult conception clearer to the Student we may further consider the matter as follows: In Kether is begun the Whirling Motion of the Universe, for it is known as the SPHERE of the PRIMUM MOBILE. This whirling combines within Itself the ideas of SELF and NOT-SELF, even as the Holy Word AL (אל— God or All) when read in **reverse** is LA (לא—Not or Ain). Yet both are but different conceptions of the ONE WORD when looked at from WITHIN OUT or from WITHOUT IN. Let us consider KETHER as the constant Whirling of these ideas ("Self and Not-self" or "God and Not"), one following the other so rapidly that neither can be affirmed or denied, we then see how KETHER becometh that Sphere in which SELFLESSNESS IS SELF.

In CHOKMAH, corresponding to the Number TWO, cometh the **realization** of this DUALITY, how by His Wisdom made He the Worlds from the Nothingness of His Own Being and how in the very CONSTANCY of this CHANGE lieth the STABILITY of the Universe. As it is written, "In Chokmah CHANGE IS STABILITY." Also in Chokmah is the reflection of the SELF of KETHER, even as in BINAH—the Third Sephira—is the reflection of Its SELF-LESSNESS. Therefore it is that the dweller in the City of the Pyramids, or BINAH, is called NEMO—No-man.

Now these THREE are ONE, KETHER-CHOKMAH-BINAH, and they form the first Triad of the Tree of Life, which is called the SUPERNAL TRIAD.

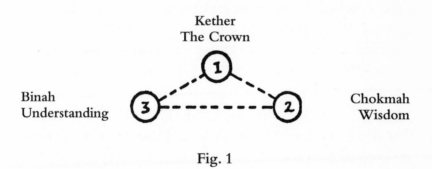

Fig. 1

The SECOND TRIAD was derived from this by REFLEXION, for as these Three are One, so this "One-in-Three" again reflected Itself, reversing as in a mirror.

Thus we obtain two further Sephiroth harmonized in a third.

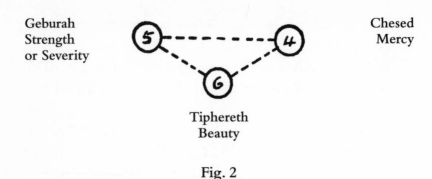

Geburah
Strength
or Severity

Chesed
Mercy

Tiphereth
Beauty

Fig. 2

The SEPHIRA CHESED, or MERCY, corresponding to the NUMBER FOUR is the reflexion of the Divine Wisdom and shows forth the Paternal and Authoritative aspect of the One as the summary of the Triple Forces of Life—the Three underlying Principles with their Central Point of Equilibrium.

The FIFTH SEPHIRA, GEBURAH or STRENGTH is the reflexion of the Enduring Quality of the Great Mother-Substance of BINAH showing forth the STRENGTH to Establish the Authority of Chesed and forming a true Balance therewith, as it is written "His **Mercy endureth** forever."[5]

These Balanced Ideas are truly Harmonized in the SIXTH SEPHIRA, which is called TIPHERETH or Beauty. For whereas it is written "Unbalanced Severity is but Cruelty and Oppression"[6] and that "Unbalanced Mercy but aids and abets evil," so in Beauty and Harmony is Eternal Truth Revealed—or Re-veiled, for Kether is Re-veiled in Tiphereth as the Father is in the Son.

Thus is the SECOND TRIAD completed and is in itself a Trinity in Unity. We thus have two TRIUNITIES of which the Second is but the reflexion of the First. But as no two ideas are complete in themselves until harmonized in a Third, so a THIRD TRIAD is essential to the previous **Two** in order to produce a TRINITY of TRINITIES or TRIADS. This then is shown as the complement of the Second or a Second Reflexion of the First Triad.

The SEVENTH SEPHIRA—Netzach, or VICTORY, shows forth more clearly the Forces of Attraction and Repulsion which were seen to be inherent in Chesed, also it symbolizes the Victory over, or Equilibrium of these forces through the Wisdom and Will which descendeth from Chokmah.

The EIGHTH SEPHIRA is called HOD, or SPLEN-DOUR, and produces the idea of VACILLATION which is secretly inherent in the Strength of Geburah through the Influence of the Selflessness of Binah. Yet this very vacillation produces a certain glittering Splendour in the fluidity of Mind and Thought.

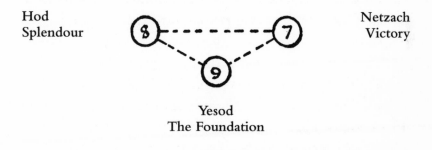

Hod
Splendour

Netzach
Victory

Yesod
The Foundation

Fig. 3

Both these again are harmonized and Established in YESOD which is the name of the NINTH SEPHIRA and means The FOUNDATION. This is the Sphere of STA-

BILITY in CHANGE even as, in the Supernal Triad, we find Chokmah is called the Sphere wherein Change is Stability.

Finally, this TRINITY of TRIADS being in itself a UNITY is Symbolized by the TENTH SEPHIRA called MALKUTH, The KINGDOM, a SINGLE SPHERE pendant to the above and summing up in itself all the foregoing qualities which it MANIFESTS according to the Creative Plan. All these qualities may be said to be Potentially inherent in KETHER—The Crown—with which MALKUTH is, in a certain Mystical sense, ONE, as it is written: "Kether is in Malkuth and Malkuth is in Kether but after another manner."[7] The NUMBER TEN attributed to Malkuth is Symbolical of the Unity returning to Zero, for even as Kether is One from Naught, so is Malkuth Naught from One—the Material Universe being, in a certain sense, the result of the Illusion of Maya, though, in another it is the Perfection of the Creative Plan, The Crowned and Conquering Child, the Pearl of Great Price, The Bride and Pride of God in his Creation.

Thus far we have mapped out very briefly the plan of the Sephiroth or NUMERICAL EMANATIONS as they are sometimes termed. It is important to note this name for the Qabalistic Plan is based on conceptions of Pure Number. All the Correspondences which may afterwards be mentioned and attributed to these TEN SEPHIROTH will have their roots in the **NUMBER** OF THE SEPHIRA corresponding, thus we may collect a hundred ideas in regard to Tiphereth, but they will all be referred to the number SIX, so that in time SIX will come to mean to us the Key of a vast storehouse of ideas. This applies to each of the other numbers of the decimal scale.

Let us now formulate more clearly the result of our researches by means of a diagram.

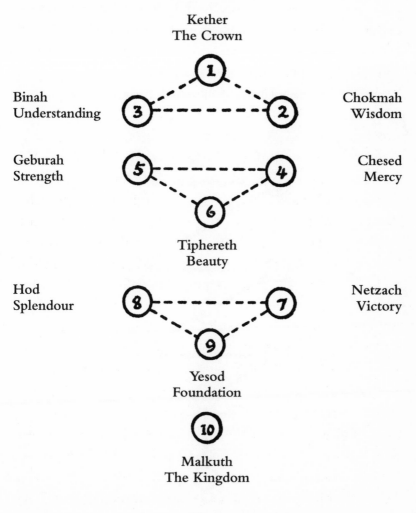

Fig. 4

This shows clearly the TRINITY of TRIADS with MALKUTH pendant to them, manifesting their Influence in the Material Universe.

Now there is another manner in which the formulation of the Ten Sephiroth emanating from the One Light may be expressed, and this, without unduly confusing the reader, I desire to show, since it illustrates in an able way the DUAL NATURE of each Sephira. This is called by the Qabalists "THE LIGHTNING FLASH" and it connects the Ten Sephiroth as shown in the following diagram.

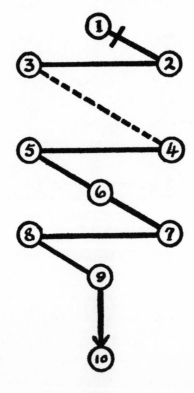

Fig. 5

It is also known as THE FLAMING SWORD, which is united with the idea of THE SERPENT of WISDOM as will be more fully explained later on.

This idea is useful as showing how each Sephira receives a certain Influence from the preceding one and in turn transmits its nature to the one following. Thus, CHOKMAH (2) may be considered as RECEPTIVE or Feminine in its relation to KETHER from which it receives a Divine Breath which becomes formulated (in Chokmah) as THE WORD or Logos, but as POSITIVE or Masculine in regard to Binah to which it transmits the WORD or WISDOM. This is in turn UNDERSTOOD, or received, by Binah from whence it is projected into Chesed, and so on,—the process apparently becoming completed in Malkuth. This is only apparent, however, since there is a certain "Method of Return" whereby the seemingly "fallen" Kingdom is once more "Raised" to the Supernal and absorbed into The Crown.

The Plan of what we have termed our "Filing Cabinet" is not, however, as yet complete. In the same way that we found a triple aspect in UNITY and that every DUALITY found its completion in a Third idea which represents its True Being, so each Sephira partakes of the nature of a TRINITY; for while we have said that each receives the influence from its predecessor in the scale of Numbers and transmits its influence to its successor, yet each is Unique in Itself and retains a certain Individuality of its own.

"MEZLA" is the name given by the Qabalists to this Influence which links together the Sephiroth and it operates not only along the course of "The Flaming Sword" but in other directions.

The following diagram will make this matter clear.

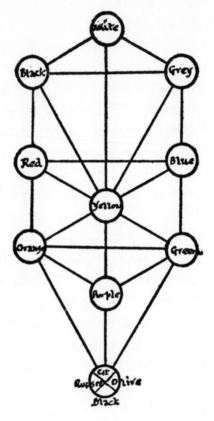

Fig. 6

It represents, as far as its structure is concerned, the COM-
PLETE PLAN of the TREE of LIFE, the details of which we
shall enlarge upon as we proceed. It is sometimes called THE
MINUTUM MUNDUM or "Little Universe of Colour"
and I shall next tell you something of the way in which its
COLOURS are derived, as by this means you will obtain a

clearer conception of the interplay of "Mezla" between the Sephiroth.

Firstly, KETHER being the Concentration of the Pure Brilliance of the Divine Light of AIN-SUPH-AUR is portrayed as WHITE.

Secondly, CHOKMAH, as the Middle Number of the first Trinity is called GREY, which is a mixture of White & Black representing all colours.

Thirdly, BINAH the last of this primary scale is BLACK or that which absorbs all colours.

The Supernal Triad is then represented as WHITE— GREY—BLACK (see plate 2 between pages 110 and 111) and these form the Roots of the Colours which follow.

The SECOND TRIAD manifests the THREE PRIMARY COLOURS **Blue**, **Red** and **Yellow** which are attributed to CHESED, GEBURAH and TIPHERETH in that order. These, as it were, draw their nature from the "King Scale" concealed in those above, as will be explained later on, viz.: Chesed blue from Chokmah, Geburah red from Binah and Tiphereth gold from Kether.

The Second Triad transmits its colour to the THIRD, its complement, by means of a mixture or blending of its rays. Thus the BLUE of CHESED combined with the YELLOW of TIPHERETH produces EMERALD GREEN in NETZACH.

The RED of GEBURAH combining with the YELLOW of TIPHERETH produces the ORANGE of HOD.

Finally the BLUE and RED of CHESED and GEBURAH produce the PURPLE of YESOD.

The Third triad in turn transmits its colours to MALKUTH in a certain Fourfold manner.

HOD and NETZACH reflect into the upper portion of Malkuth and the mixture of their colours produces a CITRINE tinge. NETZACH and YESOD produce the OLIVE GREEN portion of the Sphere. HOD and YESOD produce the RUSSET BROWN while the SYNTHESIS of all colours forms the BLACK of the lower quarter.

Thus we perceive the whole Tree vibrates between the Light and the Darkness and is composed of the Colours which naturally arise between these extremes.

It should further be noticed that the INFLUENCE or MEZLA operates so as to connect all the Sephiroth by means of TWENTY-TWO "Paths," which added to our original TEN gives in all a Thirty-Two fold classification. The SEPHER YETZIRAH an early Qabalistic Treatise, calls the whole scheme the THIRTY-TWO PATHS of WISDOM, and when so considered the Sephiroth are numbered from 1 to 10 as in our plan and the other connecting links follow from 11 to 32 as shown in the diagram. Should one read, for instance, of "The Thirty-first Path" it would mean that which connects Hod with Malkuth. This is important as it will prevent confusion later on.

It will also be apparent that the Sephiroth, in addition to receiving Influence from their immediate predecessors, as explained in diagram of the Lightning Flash, derive to some extent from each other. Thus Binah, in addition to receiving a Ray from Chokmah, receives a direct Ray from Kether, and so on (see figure 5, page 14). This difference is only apparent, however, for the influence is really inherent in the Ray received from Chokmah. On first consideration this may not be clear and the distinction is of minor importance, except as in establishing that all the qualities were inherent in the Sephiroth if considered as the result of the Lightning flash instead of under the form of the Triad. It will be seen also— for example—in the case of TIPHERETH that it receives a direct Ray from the Five preceding Sephiroth and itself HARMONIZES all of them. The same is true of Malkuth as manifesting the whole Tree.

These "Paths" or Influences, operative between the Sephiroth, are very important as a development of our Plan or "Filing Cabinet" and will be dealt with fully in the following chapters. Before completing the present section, however, it is necessary to speak of the Nature of the Ten Spheres from another aspect.

It will be remembered in regard to KETHER— The Crown—that we called it The SPHERE of the PRIMUM MOBILE for therein began the Whirling Forces which became, in turn, the cause of the System of Revolving Orbs, or Star Universe.

CHOKMAH is therefore known as THE SPHERE OF THE ZODIAC or Home of the Fixed Stars.

We next arrive at the outermost of the (then known) PLANETS, SATURN (♄), this is attributed to BINAH which is called THE SPHERE OF SATURN.

Next we find JUPITER (♃) corresponding to CHESED, while MARS (♂) is attributed to GEBURAH.

In the centre of the System is TIPHERETH which is called the SPHERE of SOL (☉), the Sun.

NETZACH and HOD correspond to VENUS (♀) and MERCURY (☿) and LUNA (☾) the Moon, is attributed to YESOD.

Finally MALKUTH is called THE SPHERE of THE ELEMENTS (Fire, Water, Air and Earth), playing upon which are the influences of all the foregoing Celestial Orbs.

The results of our study so far may be summarized as follows:

1st Triad

1	Kether	The Crown	Primum Mobile	White
2	Chokmah	Wisdom	S. of Zodiac	Grey
3	Binah	Understanding	S. of Saturn ♄	Black

2nd Triad

4	Chesed	Mercy	S. of Jupiter ♃	Blue
5	Geburah	Strength	S. of Mars ♂	Red
6	Tiphereth	Beauty	S. of Sol ☉	Yellow

3rd Triad

7	Netzach	Victory	S. of Venus ♀	Em. Green
8	Hod	Splendour	S. of Mercury ☿	Orange
9	Yesod	Foundation	S. of Luna ☾	Purple

Pendant

10	Malkuth	The Kingdom	S. of Elements	Citrine, Olive, Russet & Black

These Correspondences should be memorized with care by all students, and they should familiarize themselves with the Plan of The Tree of Life so that their minds are quite clearly impressed with its formation and parts, before proceeding with the further study of this work.

CHAPTER TWO

Concerning the Natural Basis of Correspondences in the Hebrew Alphabet

The root meaning of the Qabalah being TO RECEIVE it is essential that we be willing to receive and to MAKE OUR OWN the roots of this teaching. If Mother Earth were unwilling that the seed be properly planted in Her breast and that this seed should first of all put forth its roots into Her very being, we should not have the pleasure of seeing the Tree arising therefrom, which in due season delights us with its perfect fruits.

In the beginning of this study it is essential that the Student be receptive, and more, that he do all in his power to plant firmly the first seeds of this "Tree" in his own mind. The process may be a little dry and tedious but it is of primary importance that the details of the Plan be MEMORIZED. This is possibly the chief reason why in the early times the Qabalah was transmitted from Mouth to Ear and not in writing, for it only BEARS FRUIT in so far as it is first rooted in our minds. We may read of it, study it to some extent, juggle with it on paper, and so on, but NOT UNTIL the mind itself takes on the Image of the Tree and we are able to go, mentally from Branch to Branch, Correspondence to Correspondence, visualizing the process and thus making it a LIVING TREE, do we find that the LIGHT of TRUTH dawns upon us, and we have, as it were, succeeded in putting forth a shoot above the Earth, thus—as in the case of a young tree—finding ourselves in a new World, while yet our roots are firmly planted in our natural element.

The writer has learned this from experience. At first he could make nothing out of what seemed an unintelligible mass of Correspondences. He absorbed some of them gradually, almost sub-consciously, until after a while he began seriously to trace up one set of Correspondences. This led to further investigation. Then he tried to explain what little he knew to another, and this, as always, bore fruit, for we are often prepared to go to much greater trouble to explain an idea, than we should be willing to give to the matter for our own use. It was not until later still that the TREE began TO LIVE in him. He then found that he had been storing up the seeds of a wonderful System and that, suddenly these took almost independent life. A wonderful vista opened up, he realized that his work had not been in vain, but that which had been conceived in silence and darkness came forth a Living Child of the Light. This Child, was in a mystical sense, HIMSELF since he had begun to HARMONIZE the MICROCOSM with THE MACROCOSM and to learn the truth of the sole Hermetic Dogma "That which is above is like unto that which is below."

It is for this reason that you are urged to make these things a part of your own consciousness as early as possible, and to do so step by step as we proceed, for if you only succeed in grasping firmly the Elements of the System, you will be able to add to it for yourselves as time and experience allows.

I, who am trying to transmit what little I have grasped, am confining myself to what is already rooted in me. I shall use no books of reference while writing this, it being my intention only to give what comes readily to mind, what actually flows forth without effort. For the Qabalah is, if I may say so, a LIQUID SYSTEM. The shape of the vessel is, so to speak, shown in the "Tree" but its Stability is insured by its Change and the Influence which connects the Sephiroth must flow readily from one to another, changing as it goes, forming new combinations of ideas, and these, in turn, giving place to others which become more and more synthetic until, finally, they all merge again into the ONE.

The HEBREW alphabet is a natural basis of correspondences for every letter is NUMERICAL as well as SYMBOLICAL.

The Ten Sephiroth, to which we have already given some attention, are numbered according to the decimal system from 1 to 10. We have now to deal with the "Twenty-two Paths" which connect these Sephiroth and, as in the former instance we took for a basis of all Correspondences Pure Numbers, so the basic natures of the Paths are referred to the TWENTY-TWO LETTERS of the Hebrew Alphabet, which in turn, have a certain numerical value.

Those who are not acquainted with the SHAPES of the Hebrew letters, will find it essential to memorize them carefully, but that is not a difficult task, although it may deter some, who do not recognize the importance of having this system IN MIND rather than on paper.

For the sake of clearness on this point it is worth while to spend a little time on the study of the **shape** of these letters, so as to fix them more firmly in mind. It may cheer the reader, who enters upon this study for the first time, if I remark that the system here given out does not require a knowledge of the HEBREW LANGUAGE; the Alphabet, with its Correspondences and a few Important WORDS are all that is essential.

א

The first letter is called ALEPH and is formed א. It suggests THE SWASTIKA by shape. Its NUMERICAL value is ONE.

ב

The second letter BETH is formed ב. The shape of this letter should be carefully considered. Notice the broad line at the top tapering off on the right as it nears the base and that the broad base line projects slightly past the vertical line. I mention these details since there are other letters in the alphabet very like Beth in shape, or so they seem at first till we have grasped the characteristic details which distinguish one from another. Its NUMERICAL VALUE is TWO.

ג

The Third Letter called GIMEL is formed ג. Here again we should pay attention to its shape. It is Narrower than the previous letters, but of the same height. Notice the little rectangular piece at the base, not quite connected with the vertical line. Its NUMERICAL value is THREE.

ד

The Fourth Letter DALETH, is shaped ד. This is wider than the previous letter. The thick upper line projects slightly beyond the vertical line on the right. Its number is FOUR.

ה

The Fifth Letter is known as HÉ and is formed ה. Notice that the right-hand vertical line is a continuation of the thick upper line, but that the left-hand stroke of the letter is slightly separated from the upper horizontal line. Numerically it is FIVE.

ו

The Sixth Letter is called VAU and its form is ו. This is a narrow letter, a little like the one following, with which it should not be confused. Its Numerical value is SIX.

ז

The Seventh Letter is ZAIN shaped ז. It is a narrow letter and the vertical line is joined to the middle of the short one at top. Its value is SEVEN.

ח

The Eighth Letter is CHETH (pronounced HETH), it is formed ח. This is very like the letter HÉ, but notice the slight projections of the upper line to the right and the fact that the left vertical line meets the upper line. Its Numerical value is EIGHT.

ט

The Ninth Letter TETH is formed ט. It is a little like a serpent for which it stands symbolically. Its Numerical value is NINE.

י

The Tenth Letter is YOD formed like a simple dot י. This is said to be the basic letter of the whole alphabet and is very sacred for many reasons. It forms the characteristic parts of many of the other letters—Its value is TEN.

כ

The Eleventh Letter KAPH is shaped כ. Note the similarity to Beth the 2nd letter, the difference being that the lines form a continuous curve and there is not the projection at right of base as in Beth. Note also the Numerical value is TWENTY. (This letter has what is called a "final form" used when it comes at the end of a word. It is then shaped ך and has a numerical value of 500.)

ל

The Twelfth Letter LAMED is formed ל. It is quite a distinct type and not likely to be confused with any other letter. Its value is THIRTY.

מ

The Thirteenth Letter is MEM, מ. Do not confuse it with Teth. Its Numerical value is FORTY. This also has a "final" form. It is then written ם, but usually wider than the other letters so as not to cause confusion with one of the others called Samech. Its value is 600 when final.

נ

The Fourteenth Letter is NUN, נ. It is a narrow letter and this helps to distinguish it from Kaph, but care should be taken to avoid confusion with GIMEL. Its value is FIFTY. (Final form ן = 700 must not be confused with Vau.)

ס

The Fifteenth Letter is SAMECH—ס, it must not be confused with Mem final. Its value is SIXTY.

ע

The Sixteenth Letter is AYIN (pronounced Oyin) formed ע. Note the right-hand line forms a tail and the left-hand branch connects with it. Its Numerical value is SEVENTY.

פ

The Seventeenth Letter is PÉ its shape is פ. It is a little like Kaph but has a small tongue inside. (It means a Mouth.) Its value is EIGHTY. (Final form is ף = 800.)

צ

The Eighteenth Letter is TzADDI, צ. Note the resemblance to Ayin, but in this case the tail proceeds from the left-hand upper dot and the right-hand dot is connected with it. Its value is NINETY. (Final ץ = 900.)

ק

The Nineteenth Letter QOPH, ק is formed rather like the English P. Its value is ONE HUNDRED.

ר

The Twentieth Letter is RESH, ר. Note its similarity to Daleth, but the thick upper line curves into the vertical line without any projection. Its value is TWO-HUNDRED.

שׁ

The Twenty-first Letter is SHIN, שׁ. There is no mistaking this letter which is like a triple tongue of flame. Its value is THREE HUNDRED.

ת

The Twenty-second Letter is called TAU and is formed ת. Notice the difference between Tau, Hé and Cheth. In this case we find the left hand vertical line ends in a distinct "foot" and that it joins the top thick line. Its value is FOUR HUNDRED.

This brief description of the letters will, I trust, be useful and save confusion. We see that the Numerical values of the letters and finals give the possibility of expressing any number up to 999 by means of these Symbols. When larger numbers were necessary the letters were made LARGER so that a Large Aleph would be not One but ONE THOUSAND and so on.

I have at present made no mention of the ENGLISH equivalents as I sought to emphasize the likenesses and differences between the Hebrew letters themselves. The English correspondences will be found in the Summary Table at the end of this Chapter.

We have now to learn the SYMBOLIC meaning of the letters, for each Letter of the Hebrew, besides being a NUMBER also represents a WORD.

For instance the letter א (Aleph) can be spelled in full in Hebrew אלף, Aleph, Lamed, Pé or ALP. This word means An OX, so that we say א = an Ox. The Hebrew spelling of each letter in full is important for future study so I give this as well as the Meaning of each Word or Letter in the following Table, which should be carefully studied and memorized.

The Hebrew Alphabet

Hebrew		English	Value	Spelling	Symbol
א	Aleph	A	1	אלף	An Ox
ב	Beth	B	2	בית	House
ג	Gimel	G	3	גמל	Camel
ד	Daleth	D	4	דלת	Door
ה	Hé	H, E	5	הה	Window
ו	Vau	V, U, O	6	וו	Nail
ז	Zain	Z	7	זין	Sword
ח	Cheth	Ch	8	חית	Fence
ט	Teth	T	9	טית	Serpent
י	Yod	I, Y, J	10	יוד	Hand
כ	Kaph	K	20	כף	Palm
ל	Lamed	L	30	למד	Ox-goad
מ	Mem	M	40	מים	Water
נ	Nun	N	50	נון	Fish
ס	Samech	S	60	סמך	Prop
ע	Ayin	O or Ng	70	עין	Eye
פ	Pé	P	80	פה	Mouth
צ	Tzaddi	Tz	90	צדי	Fish-hook
ק	Qoph	Q	100	קוף	Back Head
ר	Resh	R	200	ריש	Head
ש	Shin	Sh	300	שין	Tooth
ת	Tau	Th	400	תו	Tau Cross

CHAPTER THREE

Of the Twenty-Two Paths with Their Yetziratic Attributions and Colour Correspondences

Having learned the Names and Shapes of the Letters of the Hebrew Alphabet it is now necessary to study their positions as representing the Twenty-two Paths connecting the Ten Sephiroth on the Tree of Life.

Here it may be well to state that "The Sepher Yetzirah" or "Book of Formations" allots to each of these "Paths" as well as to the "Ten Sephiroth" which it describes as "The First Ten Paths" (Making in all the Thirty-two Paths of Wisdom), a certain type of INTELLIGENCE, and though I do not consider this is of very great importance so far as the present work is concerned, we might just as well learn these titles as we proceed so as to develop our system of correspondences.

We must then deal with the Sephiroth first:
1. Kether is called "The Admirable or Hidden Intelligence."
2. Chokmah is called "The Illuminating Intelligence."
3. Binah is called "The Sanctifying Intelligence."
4. Chesed is called "The Measuring, Cohesive or Receptacular Intelligence."

5. Geburah is called "The Radical Intelligence."

6. Tiphereth is called "The Intelligence of the Mediating Influence."

7. Netzach is called "The Occult Intelligence."

8. Hod is called "The Absolute or Perfect Intelligence."

9. Yesod is called "The Pure or Clear Intelligence."

10. Malkuth is called "The Resplendent Intelligence."

So far we have disposed of the Ten Sephiroth and we shall now deal with the "Paths" which connect them.

These paths are numbered from ELEVEN to THIRTY-TWO each corresponding to a LETTER of the Hebrew alphabet shown by the leading authorities as in order from KETHER to MALKUTH.

From KETHER proceed three Paths the first of which is numbered 11 and attributed to א (Aleph) it joins Kether and Chokmah and is called the SCINTILLATING Intelligence.

12 is the Path of ב (Beth), it unites Kether and Binah and is called the Intelligence of TRANSPARENCY.

13 is the Path of ג (Gimel) it connects Kether with Tiphereth and is called the UNITING Intelligence

Three Paths proceed from CHOKMAH. The 14th is the reciprocal path uniting Chokmah with Binah. It is the path of ד (Daleth) and is called The ILLUMINATING Intelligence. The 15th, or Path of ה (Hé) joins Chokmah and Tiphereth and is called the CONSTITUTING Intelligence, and the 16th path of ו (Vau) unites Chokmah with Chesed. It is called The TRIUMPHAL or ETERNAL ONE.

Only Two Paths proceed from BINAH, the 17th uniting it with Tiphereth and attributed to ז (Zain). It is called the DISPOSING ONE or Intelligence. The 18th Path or ח

(Cheth) connects Binah with Geburah and is called The intelligence of THE HOUSE OF INFLUENCE.

Three paths proceed from Chesed. The 19th which is the reciprocal path of ט (Teth) is called the Intelligence of all the ACTIVITIES OF THE SPIRITUAL BEING. The 20th or Path of י (Yod) joins Chesed with Tiphereth and is known as the Intelligence of WILL. The 21st or Path of כ (Kaph) unites Chesed and Netzach and is called the Intelligence of CONCILIATION.

Two Paths proceed from GEBURAH. The 22nd or Path of ל (Lamed) joins Gehurah and Tiphereth. It is called the FAITHFUL Intelligence. The 23rd or Path of מ (Mem) joins Geburah and Netzach (*Editor's Note*: Achad is in error. The 23rd Path goes from Geburah to Hod.), it is known as The STABLE Intelligence.

Three Paths issue from Tiphereth. The 24th, which unites Tiphereth and Netzach is attributed to נ (Nun) and is called The IMAGINATIVE Intelligence. The 25th or Path of ס (Samech) joins Tiphereth and Yesod, it is called The Intelligence of PROBATION or TENTATIVE ONE. The 26th Path of ע (Ayin) connects Tiphereth with Netzach (*Editor's Note*: Achad is in error. The 26th Path goes from Tiphereth to Hod.) and is known as THE RENOVATING ONE.

Three Paths proceed out of Netzach. The 27th or Path of פ (Pé) is the lowest of the reciprocal paths, it unites Netzach and Hod. It is called the EXCITING Intelligence. The 28th which is called צ (Tzaddi) joins Netzach and Yesod and is known as the NATURAL Intelligence, while the 29th or Path of ק (Qoph) joining Netzach and Malkuth is called The CORPOREAL Intelligence.

The Two Paths issuing from Hod are the 30th which is that of ר (Resh) joining Hod and Yesod and called The COL-LECTING Intelligence, and the 31st Path of ש (Shin) lead-ing from Hod to Malkuth which is called The PERPETUAL Intelligence.

The 32nd or last Path is attributed to ת (Tau) it is the connecting link between Yesod and Malkuth and is called The ADMINISTRATIVE Intelligence.

Before proceeding further it is well that the Student should trace out for himself these Paths on the Diagram which follows taking notice of the manner in which the let-ters are arranged, as clearly shown thereon.

We have now what might serve as a very complete basis for our "Filing Cabinet," a Plan whereby we may express every idea in the Universe in terms of thirty-two. It will be noticed how perfectly all the parts are Balanced and Equilibrated, though we shall refer to this matter more fully when it comes to the question of making a practical attempt to deal with our own minds in this way.

Our next consideration will be to extend our series of correspondences so as to take in the Universal Ideas under-lying all Systems.

Our basis, the Hebrew Alphabet, is admirably suited to this since its 22 letters are naturally divided into three divisions which correspond with three most important Universal sets of Ideas, viz. The Elements, The Planets, and the Signs of the Zodiac.

These divisions of the Alphabet are known as the THREE Mother Letters, the SEVEN Double Letters and the TWELVE single Letters.

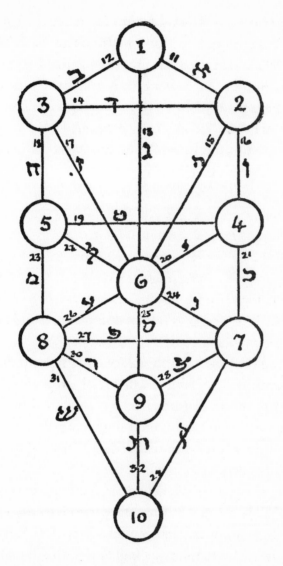

Fig. 7
Key to Plate 1 (between pages 110 and 111).

The **Three Mother Letters** are א (Aleph), מ (Mem) and ש (Shin).[1] א is attributed to Air, מ to Water and ש to Fire. The letter ת (Tau) is usually attributed to Earth although it is not a Mother letter as Earth is not a true element.

The **Seven Double Letters** (having a double sound in Hebrew) are ב, ג, ד, כ, פ, ר, ת, (B, G, D, K, P, R, Th.) They are attributed to the PLANETS as follows:

ב (Beth)	=	☿	(Mercury)
ג (Gimel)	=	☾	(Luna)
ד (Daleth)	=	♀	(Venus)
כ (Kaph)	=	♃	(Jupiter)
פ (Pé)	=	♂	(Mars)
ר (Resh)	=	☉	(Sol)
ת (Tau)	=	♄	(Saturn & Earth)

These should be memorized in connection with the Letters corresponding and they must not be confused with the SPHERES of the Planets. These planetary influences are operative in the Paths and often suggest a difference in quality from the Sephirothic Attributions. For instance Netzach, the Sphere of Venus represents rather the Sexual Love Nature, while the Path of Venus, Daleth, is the Higher Love of the Father-Mother of the Universe since the Path joins Chokmah and Binah or Wisdom and Understanding. This instance will suffice for the moment as we shall deal with the matter again later on.

The Twelve Single Letters, ה, ו, ז, ח, ט, י, ל, נ, ס, ע, צ, ק. (H, V, Z, Ch, T, I, L, N, S, O, Tz, Q.) They are attributed to the SIGNS of the ZODIAC as follows:

ה	(Hé)	=	♈	(Aries the Ram)
ו	(Vau)	=	♉	(Taurus the Bull)
ז	(Zain)	=	♊	(Gemini the Twins)
ח	(Cheth)	=	♋	(Cancer the Crab)
ט	(Teth)	=	♌	(Leo the Lion)
י	(Yod)	=	♍	(Virgo the Virgin)
ל	(Lamed)	=	♎	(Libra the Scales)
נ	(Nun)	=	♏	(Scorpio the Scorpion)
ס	(Samech)	=	♐	(Saggitarius the Archer)
ע	(Ayin)	=	♑	(Capricorn the Goat)
צ	(Tzaddi)	=	♒	(Aquarius the Waterbearer)
ק	(Qoph)	=	♓	(Pisces the Fishes)

These symbols should of course be placed on their respective Paths of the Tree of Life, and it will help the Student if he does this for himself, noticing the different Sephiroth they connect and their general relation to one another, which may at first appear somewhat puzzling on account of the Elementary and Planetary Letters and Signs coming between.

Before bringing this section to a close it will be well to explain the COLOUR SCHEME connected with the Paths, since we have already dealt with it in regard to the Ten Sephiroth.

In the simple colour scheme of the Tree of Life here used, the Colours of the Ten Sephiroth were drawn from what is called the QUEEN SCALE of Colour, while that of the Paths is derived from what is known as the KING SCALE.[2] To explain this more fully would involve a discussion of what are known as "The Four Worlds," but this we must leave till the proper place in a future chapter. Suffice it to say that a much more elaborate scheme is possible, but that this one is most convenient for our present purpose. The only thing to note is that since all is derived from the Positive and Negative aspects of the One Substance of Light, so it is fitting that the two aspects of the Tree should be represented by the interblending of the Colour Scales of the King and Queen, the Father and Mother of all things.

The Colour Scale of the Paths is obtained in a very simple and scientific manner, but this derivation is not so apparent when the colours are seen distributed over the Tree. It is therefore advisable that we trace the matter to its first principles—as our Ancient Brothers did of old—thus realizing the true significance of the Minimum Mundum or "Little Universe of Colour" (see Plate 1 between pages 110 and 111).

All the Colours of the Spectrum vibrate between the extremes of White and Black. What more natural then than that the Light should break up first into the Three Primary Colours (Attributed to the Elements and Mother Letters), then into the Seven Colours of the Rainbow (The Planetary Colours and Double Letters) and finally that these colours should blend into each other in a Twelve-fold manner. (The Signs of the Zodiac or Single letters.) Our Three, Seven and Twelve-fold division of the Letters is then the NATURAL ONE in this instance.

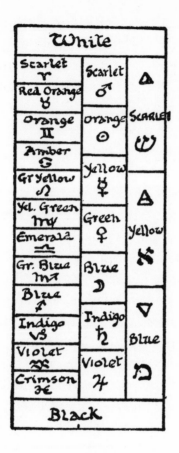

Fig. 8

CHAPTER FOUR

Concerning the Tarot Trumps and Their Attributions to the Hebrew Alphabet

There have been many false attributions of the Tarot Trumps to the Hebrew Alphabet and only one true presentation as far as I am aware. Certainly the truth was not published prior to 1909 when the Key was given in Book 777.

This is no place to attempt anything approaching a full explanation of the TAROT, but since there is a very direct correspondence between it and "The Tree of Life" it is important that the matter be at least briefly discussed.

The TARO or ROTA (meaning a Wheel) is sometimes called The Book of THOTH. It consists of 78 Leaves or Cards, divided into two main sections called the Major and Minor Arcana. The Major Arcana consists of 22 Symbolic Designs or Trumps, and these form a sort of Universal Alphabet of which many interpretations may be given.

The Minor Arcana consists of 56 Cards, 40 of which are very similar to the "small cards" of the ordinary playing pack, except that in place of Clubs, Hearts, Diamonds and Spades, we find the True Magical Weapons of the Mysteries, WANDS, CUPS, SWORDS and PENTACLES.

The remaining 16 are the Court Cards usually described as KINGS, QUEENS, KNIGHTS and PAGES, and there are 4 of each for the 4 Suits.

Properly speaking we should perhaps deal with the Minor Arcana first, but since this would necessitate a description of the Four "Worlds" of the Qabalistic Plan which I intend to treat of in the next Chapter, I shall take the 22 Trumps of the Major Arcana first and show how they correspond to the 22 Paths of the Tree and the Hebrew Alphabet.

The important thing to notice is the attribution of these cards to the Proper LETTERS of the Hebrew Alphabet, without which, all our work is awry. The cards as they are found in the pack are NUMBERED from I to XXI in Roman Numerals the remaining Trump being marked "0" or sometimes it is unnumbered.

For reasons ranging from a pledge of secrecy to gross ignorance, this Unnumbered Card has usually been placed anywhere but in the obvious position PRIOR TO NUMBER ONE, with the result that the Card Marked I, viz.: "The Magician," has been attributed to א (Aleph) and so on down the line, until the un-numbered card The Fool, was given a place. This slight change was enough to confuse the Student and prevent him from reaping the harvest of Symbolism from the Study of the Correspondences of the Tarot and Holy Qabalah, and, as we shall see later on when it comes to the question of "Climbing the Tree," it may be considered as almost criminally misleading.

Let us start then with ZERO attributing THE FOOL to the letter א (Aleph) and the path leading from Kether to Chokmah. Aleph is the letter of AIR, or the Divine Breath which arose prior to the WORD or LOGOS the Male aspect of the Creator in Chokmah.

This is THE PURE FOOL who cometh forth from the Source of LIGHT. He carries in one hand but resting on the opposite shoulder, a Staff, from which depends a wallet. He is on the verge of an Abyss, and is followed by a snapping Dog or Wolf, yet he travels "THE WAY OF THE TAO" oblivious to his surroundings. He is perhaps more properly symbolized in the Old Tarot Cards as an ANCIENT instead of a YOUNG MAN.

I have no intention of giving a description of the full symbolism of these Cards. The Reader should obtain a pack for himself and STUDY them carefully, MEDITATING on the Symbolism therein contained. He will find a Treasure House if he so do. The Modern Pack, drawn by Miss P. Coleman Smith under the direction of Mr. A. E. Waite, published by Rider and Sons, London, is the only one easy to obtain, and though the Symbolism varies somewhat from the older packs, since it is possibly the only set that can be got by the Student, I shall discuss the matter as if one were in his possession, pointing out some of the differences as we go along.

In order to avoid confusion I ask you once again to note that the TRUMPS or KEYS are numbered in ROMAN NUMERALS so that when we refer to these Trumps this will indicate the difference between them and the Numeration of the Sephiroth, Paths or values of the letters of the Alphabet.

I. The MAGICIAN = ב (Beth) = Mercury who is clearly the God of Magick. This card shows The Magician with the

4 Symbolic Elemental Weapons on his table. He makes the Sign Solvé et Coagula, viz.: he points upwards and downwards as if to indicate "That which above is like unto that which is below and that which is below is like that which is above for the performance of the Miracle of the ONE SUBSTANCE." This card is given (Bk. 777) the Title of THE MAGUS OF POWER.

II. The HIGH PRIESTESS = ג = Gimel = The Moon. This card shows the Priestess seated between Two Pillars representing Severity and Mercy which are Established in Strength by means of Equilibrium. This, however, is said not to be the correct Symbolism as the Pillars of The Tree of Life have their Heads in Chesed and Geburah while The Supernal Triad forms an Arch over them. Since The High Priestess is attributed to the Path from Kether to Tiphereth, she would partake of the Nature of the Supernals and should then be ABOVE rather than BETWEEN the Pillars. Notice however that The MOON is at her feet, which shows clearly her correspondence with Gimel, the Letter of the Moon, and also indicates how much mistaken we might have been had we attributed Aleph to the Magician, for then Beth would have been the High Priestess who is hardly symbolic of Mercury. Again she would then be on the path from Kether to Binah and the Pillar Symbolism would not be explained nor the Luna Crescent. Notice she has the Scroll of the Law, ThORA, on her lap, and these letters signify TARO and ROTA. She is said to represent The Holy Guardian Angel and is given the title of PRIESTESS OF THE SILVER STAR.

III. The EMPRESS = ד = Daleth = Venus is attributed to the reciprocal Path from Chokmah to Binah. The Card shows the symbol of Venus on her shield, another proof of the correctness of the attributions. She is Crowned with Twelve Stars, thus combined with the high Priestess, whose Path is crossed by this one, (note the "cross" on breast of H. P.) we have a Symbol of Our Lady Babalon, Crowned with the Stars and with the Moon at Her feet. The title of this card is THE DAUGHTER OF THE MIGHTY ONES.

IV. The EMPEROR = ה = Aries. Notice the Rams Heads on his throne. He is called THE SUN OF THE MORNING—CHIEF AMONG THE MIGHTY ONES.

V. THE HIEROPHANT = ו = Taurus, The Bull, Osiris the Initiator into the Mysteries in the Old Aeon. Title: The MAGUS OF THE ETERNAL.

VI. THE LOVERS = ו = Gemini. The Symbolism of the older packs is better in this instance as they show a Man between Two Women, one of which represents Virtue and the other Vice, or better a Virgin and a Harlot. Above is seen Cupid with his bow and arrow. The card signifies the necessity of overcoming prejudice regarding the so-called opposites. The title is THE CHILDREN OF THE VOICE; THE ORACLES OF THE MIGHTY GODS.

VII. THE CHARIOT = ה = Cancer. The Symbolism of this card is best studied in the Design given by Eliphas Levi in Le Dogme et Rituel de la Haute Magie. It represents the harnessing of the pairs of Opposites, or Black and White Sphinxes and, of course, a great deal more. Title: THE CHILD OF THE POWERS OF THE WATERS; THE LORD OF THE TRIUMPH OF LIGHT.

VIII. STRENGTH = ט = Leo. This card is sometimes called "Fortitude." Notice the Lion and Serpent Symbolism

(Leo = The Lion, Teth = The Serpent). A Woman is seen opening the Jaws of Lion, the Old pack shows her closing them. Title: THE DAUGHTER OF THE FLAMING SWORD.

IX. THE HERMIT = ' = Virgo. An Ancient is seen carrying a Lamp and Staff, the old pack shows lamp concealed by his cloak to represent Secrecy. He is said to be "The Fool" of the Path of Aleph bringing Light to the College of Adepts. He is styled THE MAGUS OF THE VOICE OF POWER.

X. THE WHEEL OF FORTUNE = כ = Jupiter. A very important Symbol the title of which is THE LORD OF THE FORCES OF LIFE. This will be dealt with more fully in another chapter. In fact, I give the interpretation of the cards very briefly, since the symbolism of the Paths is more important when considered from the BOTTOM TO THE TOP OF THE TREE, as that of the Sephiroth is from the TOP TO THE BOTTOM, for the "Flaming Sword" or "Lightning Flash" descended, but the Paths were formed by the ASCENT OF THE SERPENT OF WISDOM. The Wheel, in a way, indicates this eternal ascent and descent.

XI. JUSTICE = ל = Libra. (Note. In the old packs this card is numbered VIII and STRENGTH XI. This has been corrected in Rider's Pack.) The Card shows a figure with Sword and Balances which clearly indicates Libra. Title— DAUGHTER OF THE LORDS OF TRUTH, the RULER OF THE BALANCES.

XII. The HANGED MAN = מ = Water. Title: —THE SPIRIT OF THE MIGHTY WATERS. Note: This card should show—according to some authorities—a man hanging from a gallows shaped like the letter ד (Daleth)—His legs, arms and head symbolizing a Cross above an inverted triangle. He is said to be the Adept suspended over THE ABYSS thus bringing down the LIGHT as the Redeemer.

XIII. DEATH = נ = Scorpio. Old card shows skeleton with Scythe mowing down Heads which grow again as fast as they are cut down. Viz.: Death is the Gate of Life and Love. Title—THE CHILD OF THE GREAT TRANSFORMERS, THE LORD OF THE GATES OF DEATH.

XIV. TEMPERANCE = ס = Saggitarius. Design should show, it is said, symbolism of the Waters of Chesed descending upon the Fires of Netzach, and the Fire of Geburah uniting with the Water of Hod. Title: —THE DAUGHTER OF THE RECONCILERS, THE BRINGER FORTH OF LIFE.

XV. THE DEVIL = ע = Capricorn. Again one should refer to Eliphas Levi's design for the true Symbolism of this Card which, as a rule is much misunderstood. The Pentagram on Forehead should not be "reversed" as in Rider's Pack and there should be a Flaming Torch between his horns etc. Title: THE LORD OF THE GATES OF MATTER, THE CHILD OF THE FORCES OF TIME.

XVI. THE BLASTED TOWER = פ = Mars. It is sometimes called The Destruction of the House of God, and it conceals symbolism of Initiation. Title: THE LORD OF THE HOSTS OF THE MIGHTY.

XVII. THE STAR = צ = Aquarius. The Figure in this Card suggests the Swastika. Symbolism should be carefully studied. Title—THE DAUGHTER OF THE FIRMAMENT, THE DWELLER BETWEEN THE WATERS. I had written thus far (May 31st, 1922 E.V.) when I was rewarded with the opening up of SECRETS so wonderful that they have changed my whole conception of the Plan of the Qabalah, and have indeed proved not alone a LIGHTNING FLASH to destroy THE HOUSE OF GOD but a SERPENT of WISDOM to re-construct it, and yet again a STAR which explains all SYMBOLISM. This matter being of such TRANSCENDENT IMPORTANCE will be dealt with in the form of Appendixes to this Volume which will be obtainable under certain special conditions. Meanwhile the main plan of this book will be followed as originally intended, since it is necessary that the Student should have a clear and comprehensive grasp of the old system before he could appreciate the New.

XVIII. THE MOON = ק = Pisces. This card is very interesting and is understood to represent the ILLUSION of the MOON consciousness with its constant change. Two Towers are shown with a narrow winding path between. Above is a strange Moon, below are two dogs or jackals barking at it and below that again a Pool from which issues a Crab or Crayfish symbolical of Kephra the Rising Sun. Title: THE RULER OF FLUX AND RE-FLUX, THE CHILD OF THE SONS OF THE MIGHTY.

XIX. THE SUN = ר = The Sun. Here we have a truly magnificent Symbol though it is better expressed in the old packs where in front of a wall TWO CHILDREN Embrace beneath the Rays of the SUN. Rider's Pack shows THE CHILD on THE WHITE HORSE, the Crowned and Conquering Child Prophesied in Revelations and to be manifested in this New Aeon.

XX. THE LAST JUDGMENT = ש = Fire. Here we have the "Stelé of the Old Aeon" Gabriel Blowing His Trumpet and the Dead rising from their tombs. Those who know of the Fire of the Holy Spirit have nothing to fear from this event. The Gross must pass through the Fire however, as they need the refining which will make it possible for them to pass on to the Second Order where they will next be tried in INTELLECT as shown in Liber Legis. Shin (ש) it must be remembered is both FIRE and SPIRIT. The card suggests Regeneration. "This is my body which I destroy in order that it may be renewed."

XXI. THE UNIVERSE = ת = Saturn is called THE GREAT ONE OF THE NIGHT OF TIME. This last trump of the pack is a Symbol of the Universe. It contains symbolism of the Ellipse, the Squaring of the Circle, etc. It represents, in a measure, the Daughter (Malkuth) who is to be RAISED to the THRONE of the MOTHER. One interpretation reads "And in the heart of the Sphinx danced the Lord Adonai, in His garlands of roses and pearls making glad the concourse of things; yea, making glad the concourse of things." So be it My Lord ADONAI.

We have now dealt very briefly with the Major Arcana of the Tarot, but please understand this is quite useless until the Student applies himself carefully to the Study of the Cards themselves, makes himself quite familiar with the designs and places them on the "Tree of Life" in the order indicated by the letters and the paths as heretofore described. Then only will he begin to realize the great importance of these symbols as a means of SELF-INITIATION, and as part

of the great system of Correspondences which he is building up into that "FILING CABINET" which in the end
will be found to be "THE TEMPLE OF THE LIVING
GOD."

CHAPTER FIVE

Being Some Account of the Ineffable Name and of the Four Worlds with Their Correspondences to the Minor Arcana of the Tarot

We must now consider what the Qabalists have to say in regard to the "Four Worlds" which are under the dominion of the Ineffable Name of Four Letters יהוה IHVH usually called Tetragrammaton.

There are three methods of classifying these "Four Worlds":

1. We may consider them as upon Four Planes one above the other, that is to say, we can take our "Tree of Life" and imagine that there are three similar "Trees" occupying the same position except that each represents a different Level. We can then easily adjust our conception to the consideration of Four Worlds, occupying the same space, but being of different grades of substance, one interpenetrating the other.

2. We may consider "Four Trees" placed vertically one above the other so that the Kether of the First "Tree" corresponds with the Malkuth of the one above, and so on, thus obtaining a ground plan of all four.

3. We may consider the One "Tree" we have already studied as divided into Four Parts in a particular manner to be discussed later.

These three methods are useful for different purposes and we should adopt the most convenient for our special needs. I may mention that when a very minute classification is desirable the Sephiroth in each of the Four Worlds can each in turn be divided into "ten" by placing a small complete Tree of Life in each Sephira, thus we should obtain 400 different Sephiroth and a very great number of "Paths." But this is too complex for our present purpose.

The Names of the Four Worlds are: ATZILUTH, BRIAH, YETZIRAH and ASSIAH.

1. ATZILUTH, the Highest, is the ARCHETYPAL WORLD. It is in this World that the Primal Ideas arose in the Mind of THE FATHER, Who through WISDOM was able to comprehend the Silent Voice of the One Existence. These were the "Seed Ideas" as yet unmanifest, but containing Potentially the WILL of the Father to manifest in a suitable Substance. This World is attributed to the First letter of the Ineffable Name ' IVD the Letter of the FATHER.

2. BRIAH is the CREATIVE WORLD which, being impregnated with the Will or Life, of the Father is a LIVING SUBSTANCE, Understanding what is necessary to the gradual formation of the ideas and the preparation and bearing of them until perfectly fashioned It is therefore referred to the Second Letter of the Name, ה, Hé, The Great Mother.

3. YETZIRAH is the FORMATIVE WORLD, the product of the previous two, where the perfected ideas having

taken form, await a suitable material body in which to clothe them. It is the world of Symbols something like the Plan of the Great Architect ready for execution. It is attributed to the letter ו which is that of the SON.

4. ASSIAH is the MATERIAL WORLD wherein all these former worlds of fine matter are Materialized and Manifested in tangible form. It is the Universe as we know it through the five senses. This is attributed to the Final ה which is called the DAUGHTER and is usually written with a dot in the centre to distinguish it from The Mother.

Now these Worlds are symbolized by the FOUR SUITS in the TAROT viz.: WANDS, CUPS, SWORDS and PENTACLES. Notice how closely the symbolism follows, Wands, the Vertical Lines of Will correspond to The Father, Cups hollow and receptive are the Understanding or The Mother, Swords formed as a Cross, the vertical combined with the horizontal, are equivalent to the Son, while Pentacles are the Materialized Daughter summing up all the foregoing.

There are 40 of these small cards, ten of each suit in turn numbered from One (or Ace) to Ten. These connect at once with the Ten Sephiroth. The Four Aces belong to Kether, the Four Twos to Chokmah, etc., until the four Tens are attributed to Malkuth. If we arrange these cards in Ten packs in the form of the "Tree of Life," placing the Wands uppermost, then the Cups below them and the Swords below that and the Pentacles lowest of all, we find we have a clear set of symbols for the Four Worlds. For instance, we pick up The Six of Cups, what does that mean? Why, 6 is Tiphereth and Cups = Briah, so we obtain Tiphereth in the Creative World.

Again Four of Swords will be Chesed of Yetzirah, The Mercy
of the Formative World. This is so simple that it needs no
further explanation.

Now we should note that the Ineffable name יהוה is
particularly attributed to the FOUR ELEMENTS, Jehovah
being, as we shall see later on, the God of the Elements. Now
י is FIRE, ה is Water, ו is Air and the final ה is Earth. Again we
find the same symbolism. The fire of the Father, the Water
of the Great Sea or Mother, coming together and forming Air,
the Son, which with the previous two produces Earth, the
Daughter. These again correspond with the Tarot Symbols,
Wands = Fire, Cups = Water, Swords = Air and Pentacles =
Earth.

We should now consider the Third method of attributing the FOUR WORLDS to the TREE of LIFE. In this we
find a peculiar arrangement. KETHER, the CROWN, being
PURE EXISTENCE, the Qabalists designated IT אהיה
AHIH which means EXISTENCE IS EXISTENCE. This
has been translated in the Scriptures as I AM THAT I AM.
Kether is Pure Unity and LIGHT, from which cometh LIFE
which is the Substance of Light, and this being a LIVING
SUBSTANCE is divided into the FATHER or LIFE and
THE MOTHER or SUBSTANCE. But these three are One
in Light and form the Supernal Triad KETHER,
CHOKMAH, BINAH. Now the Qabalists attribute י of
יהוה to Chokmah and ה to Binah as these are the FATHER-
MOTHER of all things. They sometimes say that the top-
most point of the Yod is in Kether and represents AHIH.
Now ו Vau, the third Letter or SON is attributed to
TIPHERETH and the SON ruleth over the Six Sephiroth,

Chesed, Geburah, Tiphereth, Netzach, Hod and Yesod; otherwise the Moral or Intellectual part of the Tree. Again the final ה or Daughter is assigned to MALKUTH the Kingdom, which is the materialized Manifestation of the foregoing. She is sometimes called The Queen as the Son is called The King who is Crowned by Kether, but this may perhaps cause some confusion with the Tarot, so we had better designate The FATHER as THE KING, THE MOTHER as THE QUEEN, THE SON as the PRINCE and the DAUGHTER as the PRINCESS.

We now come to the question of the COURT CARDS of the TAROT and we find FOUR of these for each of the FOUR SUITS. They are named, on the Cards, KINGS, QUEENS, KNIGHTS and PAGES. It is evident that there is a connection here with the Ineffable Name, but there has been some confusion in the Symbolism of the Cards for we find the Kings seated on Thrones or in Chariots, the Queens on Thrones, the Knights on Horses and the Pages are on foot. Now the Force of the FATHER (or KING) is QUICK, SUDDEN and very ACTIVE as is the Male Generative Power and this is best symbolized by the HORSED FIGURES who are borne rapidly forward with rush and energy. THESE then are the true KINGS and representatives of the forces of ' in the Name. The QUEENS are as they should be, seated upon THRONES as if to signify the ENDURING quality of the MOTHER who waits passively while the result of the Active force is at work within her. The cards marked Kings are the real PRINCES or representatives of ו The Son, for they are seated in CHARIOTS drawn by Horses (or should be so shown) and thus they represent the

Combined action of the Father and Mother, somewhat less swift than the Father and more active than the Mother. The Pages are the true PRINCESSES or Daughters. Standing alone because they manifest the FATHER, MOTHER and SON, but only powerful insofar as they remember whence they came. The FOUR KINGS then belong to CHOKMAH, the FOUR QUEENS to BINAH, the FOUR PRINCES to TIPHERETH and the FOUR PRINCESSES to MALKUTH. There being 4 Suits these are particularly referred to the ELEMENTS in the case of the Court Cards, though as before there is a correspondence with the "Four Worlds" if we use the First Classification of Different PLANES.

The KING of WANDS, for instance, is called The LORD of The FLAME and the LIGHTNING, the KING of the SPIRITS of FIRE[1] for The KING is the Father ('), and WANDS are attributed to FIRE. So, again, the KING of CUPS is known as The Lord of the Waves and the Waters, the King of the Hosts of the Sea. But let me remind you once again that these KINGS are marked as "Knights" on the cards themselves. It is advisable that the true titles be written on the cards by the student.

We may also obtain a very complete Sub-elemental Attribution to these Court cards, for The KINGS being ' forces are all FIERY while there are FOUR SUITS also attributed to the elements, so we get different combinations as follows—the King of Wands is FIRE of FIRE, King of Cups = FIRE of WATER, King of Swords = FIRE of AIR and King of Pentacles = FIRE of EARTH. So also with all the other cards. The Prince of Cups, for instance, is AIR of

WATER because the Prince = ו = Air, and Cups = ה = Water. This may appear a little confusing at first but one soon grasps the idea and once it is fixed in the mind one has the first principles of all this symbolism firmly rooted in consciousness.

There is however another consideration which should be brought forward, viz.: That KETHER is PURE SPIRIT so that the NAME יהוה really only governs the NINE SEPHIROTH below Kether, for in a certain manner, as mentioned before, it is representative of THE ELEMENTS ONLY, and these are CROWNED by SPIRIT. MAN, too, is made up of these ELEMENTS, but by the LIGHT of THE HOLY SPIRIT within him he may RULE and GOVERN them once he has COME TO THE LIGHT or found the KINGDOM of HEAVEN within himself. The process whereby he may find his TRUE SELF will be described later on, but here we should remark that when he does so, he escapes the LAW of the FOUR—the Cross or Square—and becomes a Perfect MICROCOSM or LITTLE UNIVERSE made in the Image and Likeness of GOD. Then he is Symbolized by the PENTAGRAM or FIVE-POINTED STAR of UNCONQUERED WILL and Mystically the letter ש, which is the HOLY SPIRIT, is said to descend into יהוה thus forming יהשוה or Jeheshuah, the God-Man. This process is symbolized in the Tarot by the ACES which correspond to KETHER and SPIRIT being placed at the top of a Pentagram, the other four arms being attributed to FIRE, WATER, AIR and EARTH, also to KINGS, QUEENS, PRINCES and PRINCESSES. Thus we find we have FIVE ELEMENTS or rather FOUR ELEMENTS which have their ROOTS in SPIRIT. The Aces are called the ROOTS of the Elements, thus, Ace of Wands = The Root of Fire, Ace of Cups = the Root of Water, Ace of Swords = the Root of Air and the Ace of Pentacles = the Root of Earth. These ROOTS signify the SPIRIT. All the foregoing will be made clearer if we complete this Chapter by summing up what we have said in tabular form and also by means of a diagram showing the Holy Pentagram, or Man, with the Elements rightly attributed according to THE NAME יהשוה.

THE FOUR WORLDS

4	3	2	1
ASSIAH	YETZIRAH	BRIAH	ATZILUTH
Material	Formative	Creative	Archetypal
ה Hé H	ו Vau V	ה Hé H	י Yod Y
Earth	Air	Water	Fire
PENTACLES	SWORDS	CUPS	WANDS
(Malkuth)	(Tiphereth)	(Binah)	(Chokmah)

This gives the attributions of small cards.

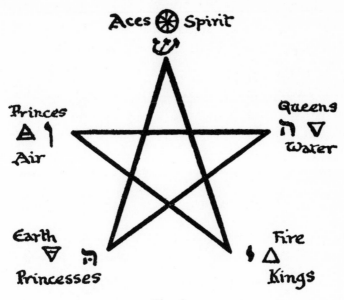

Fig. 9

י	= I	Kings (on Horses)	Fire	Chokmah
ה	= H	Queens (thrones)	Water	Binah
ש	= Sh	Aces (Roots)	Spirit	Kether
ו	= V	Princes (Chariots)	Air	Tiphereth
ה	= H	Princesses (Foot)	Earth	Malkuth

CHAPTER SIX

Concerning the Macrocosm and the Microcosm and How by Means of the Tree of Life We May Learn to Unite Them

We have spoken in the last chapter of the Microcosm which is Man, we must now discuss the Macrocosm which is God, and the Means of Uniting these which is called the Great Work.

When the Qabalists tell us of the Creation of the Universe through the Father, Mother, Son and Daughter symbolized in the NAME יהוה, which is active in the SEPHIROTH, we must not think that the process ends with the production of MALKUTH, the Material World, for this is likened to the UNREDEEMED or Animal Soul in Man, viz: that which only Perceives and Feels. This "fallen one" must be RAISED TO THE THRONE OF THE MOTHER, that is to say, come to UNDERSTAND. The process of redemption is symbolised as follows, The DAUGHTER must marry the SON, she then becomes THE MOTHER who in turn arouses the active force of THE FATHER, and these twain being UNITED, all is RE-ABSORBED into THE

CROWN. This sounds complicated, but it is very important that we should grasp its true meaning.

HERMES tells us "That which is above is like unto that which is below, and that which is below is like that which is above, for the performance of the Miracle of the One Substance."[1] The Qabalists say that The Universe is the MACROCOSM and that Man is the MICROCOSM or Little Universe. Between these is a direct CORRESPON-DENCE for Man is made in the Image and Likeness of God. We are all produced from the ONE SUBSTANCE and have within us, potentially, all the possibilities and Powers of Nature and of God, but these have to be brought out and developed before we can say we have become the perfect Microcosm, a true Mirror of the ALL. We are, at first, like the Unredeemed Daughter, creatures of mere animal feeling with some power of perception. We have within us a vast storehouse, the AUTOMATIC or SUBCONSCIOUS part of our being, which corresponds to YESOD the FOUNDATION on the Tree of Life. This Automatic Consciousness takes care of the vital functions of the body, without need of attention from the conscious self, which is, after all, but a very limited thing and mostly illusion at that. Now the SON, with the Sephiroth which He represents, corresponds in man to the REASON and INTELLECT, and their Marriage with the lower or animal soul is necessary for our development, but there is a further Mystery, for above REASON lies another state, THE SUPERCONSCIOUS, which alone brings UNDER-STANDING. But we have to go through certain processes, pass certain ordeals, before this CHILD of the HIGHER is born in us. When we UNDERSTAND we shall be able to perceive directly, without inference or deduction, and in that state we may receive the TRUE WISDOM OF THE FATHER, and so regain the LIGHT of THE CROWN.

This is a very brief statement, but it will give some idea of the necessity for "CLIMBING THE TREE OF LIFE" which is the Road to the Attainment of ADEPTSHIP, leading in turn to the perfection of the MASTERS, who have completed the GREAT WORK as far as they Themselves are concerned.

Just as the Microcosm—Man—is symbolized by the Pentagram or Five Pointed Star, so is the MACROCOSM —GOD—symbolized by the HEXAGRAM or SIX-FOLD STAR. The attainment of "Union with God" is considered by all religions to be the Great Work which lies before us. We may symbolize this as Uniting the FIVE and the SIX, and this operation is sometimes called $5° = 6^\square$ which is the formula used by the Great Brotherhood known as the A∴A∴ This particular stage belongs to the Grade called Adeptus Minor, and corresponds to the "Knowledge and Conversation of the Holy Guardian Angel" or True Self, which is obtained in TIPHERETH, where the DAUGHTER is united to the SON. In order to make this clear I must describe some of the necessary steps leading to this Attainment.

The TREE of LIFE is sometimes considered as representing the GRADES of a THREE-FOLD ORDER, in which case each SEPHIRA is attributed to one Grade, or represents the stage of the work attained to by those who hold that Grade. We must remember that each Sephira is both Positive and Negative, so likewise is this Order a CHAIN SYSTEM wherein those holding any Grade receive an influx of help from the Grade above them and transmit their help in turn to those below. Thus there is an unbroken stream of INFLUENCE from the CROWN to the KING-DOM and beyond.

Suppose one aspires to climb this TREE, how important it becomes that he should know the Correspondences, Symbols, etc., which are the Land Marks and Sign Posts on the Way. Do not think that I have given you all the Correspondences, there are hundreds of them to each Sephira and Path, but I have given you enough to show the main idea, and you will find the means of extending your knowledge in such books as 777 (which is a complete Table of these Correspondences,) and elsewhere. This treatise is intended only to indicate something of the Nature and Use of the Tree of Life, and so I have only dealt with the different aspects very briefly. Each would require volumes in order to cover the subject fully.

I will now tell you something of the Order whereby one may learn the Path to the Highest. First one becomes a PRO-BATIONER, that is, one who is outside the Order but who is OBLIGATED to "Obtain a Scientific Knowledge of the Nature and Powers of his own being."[2] When he has accomplished this task he becomes a NEOPHYTE and enters the Sphere of MALKUTH. There he learns to CONTROL the Nature and Powers of his own being. He finds these much wider than he expected and his task before reaching YESOD is to control the ASTRAL PLANE, which he accomplishes by the use of the Pentagram which makes it possible either to Invoke or Banish all the Elements and to control them. In YESOD he becomes a ZELATOR and must learn to CON-

TROL the FOUNDATIONS of his own being. This is
accomplished through control of the body and breath or
Prana. On passing to HOD the Sphere of Mercury he
becomes a PRACTICUS and must overcome the VACIL-
LATIONS of his own being. He studies the Holy Qabalah
and such Eastern Systems as Gnana Yoga. In NETZACH he
becomes a PHILOSOPHUS, and his task is to obtain CON-
TROL of the ATTRACTIONS and REPULSIONS of his
own being. Netzach being the sphere of Venus and the House
of Love he does so by means of proper DEVOTION or in
Eastern Systems BHAKTI YOGA. Thus, having passed the
Initiations of the 4 Elements, he is ready to pass on to the
INNER ORDER which lies behind the VEIL. This is called
the College of Adepts or COLLEGIUM AD SPIRITUM
SANCTUM, but he must wait outside the Veil until he has
transmuted his previous work into Spirit, that is to say, he
must obtain DHYANA the sixth stage of Raja Yoga as it is
called in the East, or, as we call it, he must ATTAIN to THE
KNOWLEDGE and CONVERSATION of THE HOLY
GUARDIAN ANGEL which is his Task in TIPHERETH.
While in the Grade of ADEPTUS MINOR, he learns the
True Mysteries of the Rosy Cross, so that his task in the next
Grade, ADEPTUS MAJOR, corresponding to GEBURAH,
is to apply the FORMULA of the R. C. Thus he becomes
a true Magician if he uses his Powers rightly. After accom-
plishing this task he becomes an EXEMPT ADEPT and
passes to CHESED, the Sphere of Jupiter, where he must
exercise his authority in the right way, for he has attained to
all that is possible on the Plane of Reason. Again he must
wait before he passes to the Third Order, for there is indeed

a Great Gulf Fixed between Chesed and Binah and this is called THE ABYSS. Strange as it may seem he must give up all he has attained, including himself, before he can pass this Abyss and be re-born of the Spirit into BINAH where he becomes known as NEMO or No-Man. He is now MASTER of THE TEMPLE for having given up 'self' he is able to comprehend and Understand ALL. CHOKMAH the next SPHERE is attributed to the GRADE of MAGUS. Here we find the Great Masters of Wisdom, those who are truly WORDS (Logoi) under Whose WILL all below is directed, and HUMANITY gradually INITIATED, according to the Plan of the ONE CREATOR and by the LIGHT of THE CROWN. The highest Grade, is called IPSISSIMUS, it is that wherein SELFLESSNESS is SELF and EXISTENCE IS EXISTENCE, of which no word may he spoken.

Thus have I briefly mapped out the Way. It is for you to discover The Truth and to Live the Life.

I have made no mention of the "Paths" which connect the Sephiroth, and which correspond to the Symbolic Designs of the TARO. I will however indicate the method of progress from Grade to Grade. From Malkuth to Yesod there is but one "path" to travel. From YESOD to HOD there are two, for it is necessary to combine the ideas suggested in the paths from MALKUTH to HOD with those from YESOD to HOD. Again from HOD to NETZACH there are "three" to be combined;—the Path from Malkuth to Netzach, the one from Yesod to Netzach and that which leads directly from Hod to Netzach. Thus, step by step, one must discover the Way, Pass the Ordeals and Tests, Overcome his own Obstacles and Illusions. (Though there are Those who will help us if we truly aspire and are prepared always to GIVE HELP in our turn.)

Every step we take, we must retain our link with the Higher and with the Lower, for this is an endless chain and every link is tested to the uttermost lest that chain break. Or again, it is called the Great Wheel of Life, the least little "cog" of which may well be proud in trying to fulfil his office perfectly.

CHAPTER SEVEN

Concerning the Literal Qabalah and the Methods of Gematria, Notaricon and Temurah

So far we have dealt solely with "The Tree of Life" and its "Correspondences," making no mention of what is known as the "Literal Qabalah." This, however, plays an important part in our studies and workings.

The Hebrew Alphabet, as previously explained, has a numerical basis, so that, in truth, every Word as well as every Letter is really expressive of a number. Again, any two Words having a similar Numerical Value may be said to have a natural affinity through their vibration. This is the basic idea of what is called GEMATRIA and upon it a system of interesting Correspondences has been built up, especially in regard to the Hebrew Scriptures and other Qabalistic writings, wherein a Word or even a Sentence may be made to disclose some hidden meaning (often concealed in that way by the writer) by finding the numerical correspondence between it and other words or sentences of like value.

To take a very simple example in the case of the "Motto" of the writer which is אחד = ACHAD meaning UNITY. This will be found to add to 13, thus א = 1, ח = 8, ד = 4;—

1+8+4 = 13, whereas the word אהבה, AHBH, meaning Love or Beloved has the same value thus: א = 1, ה = 5, ב = 2, ה = 5; 1+5+2+5 = 13. The close correspondence between these two ideas or words, is quite plain.

The above is a very simple example, there are of course others not so apparent, but of great interest to Students of the Q. B. L. Of particular value is the correspondence between the Letter ש = 300 and the words רוח אלהים RUCh ALHIM, Ruach Elohim, "The Spirit, or Breath, of the Creative Gods," for these words add to 300 also. Again ש = 300 = מם, יוד, הי, למד, אלף, (ALP, LMD, HI, IVD, MM) the word ALHIM with each letter spelt in full. Also we find the words בפאהה אור which are equivalent to "Khabs am Pekht" or "Light in Extension" have a numerical value of 300 which brings out their correspondence with the Letter of Spirit and Fire ש.

Now ALHIM is the word for "The Creative Gods" mentioned in the First Verse of Genesis which reads "In the Beginning ALHIM created the essence of the Heavens and the essence of the Earth." ALHIM has the value of 86, א = 1, ל = 30, ה = 5, י =10, מ = 40 = 86, and this is also the numeration of אהיה אדני AHIH ADNI which means "I AM ADONAI," Adonai is the Lord who is said to have been one with all the Works of the Creator and is, so to speak, The Holy Guardian Angel of Humanity.

The first Word of Genesis BRAShITh has been commented upon so fully by Qabalistic Scholars that I shall make no attempt to do so in this place. Enough has been said to give an idea of the methods employed in this type of working, except that we may also obtain the "Key Note" of Words through their TAROT correspondences, after having reduced their number to its essence by means of "Theosophical Addition." Thus, we take the Hebrew Word תששימ =400+300+40+10+300 = 1050 and after adding the digits of this number 1+0+5+0 = 6 we may refer it to the VIth Key of the Tarot, which proves to be THE LOVERS. Since the Hebrew Word referred to happens to mean "coition" we find an instance where the Tarot may throw valuable light on the matter and is the Key to the meaning of the Word. Again 6, its basis, is suggestive of the Interlaced Triangles or the Hexagram, which represents the Marriage of Fire and Water, or The Father and Mother. So then we obtain another interpretation by means of a SYMBOL. Further 6 = ו (Vau) the letter of the SON in the Ineffable Name יהוה and this SON is the result of the Union of the Father and Mother, which is in turn true numerically, since י = 10 and, ה = 5, 10+5 = 15, 1+5 = 6= ו. This example will suffice, but the student will be able to trace many others of equal or greater interest.

Another Qabalistic Method is called NOTARICON, meaning a Shorthand-writer.

In this case the Initial, Final or Medial Letters of a Word, are taken as the Initial letters of the Words of a Sentence which has an affinity with the original Word. Thus, to use a well known example, BRAShITh, the first word of Genesis is made to suggest the Sentence BRAShITh RAH ALHIM ShIQBLV IShRAL ThVRH, which means "In the Beginning Elohim saw that Israel would accept the Law." There are many other possible sentences to be formed from these Initial Letters as will be found in the various treatises on this subject.

On the other hand, sometimes the Initials of a Sentence are used to form a Word, as in the case of the phrase ATEH GIBOR LEOHM ADONAI, expressed in the Word of Power, AGLA, which then may be said to conceal the Meaning of the whole sentence "Unto Thee be the Power O My Lord Adonai." Another well known example is ChKMH NSThRH, which expresses the SECRET WISDOM of the Qabalah, the Initials ChN (Chen) forming the Hebrew Word for GRACE.

There are also many methods of "permutation" or TEMURAH of which one is known as ANBM (Anbam). The Hebrew Alphabet is divided into two halves of eleven letters each, the top half in its usual order (from Right to Left) and the lower reversed. Various arrangements form different combinations. In the case of ANBM the lower line appears thus:

11	10	9	8	7	6	5	4	3	2	1
K	I	T	Ch	Z	V	H	D	G	B	A
S	O	P	Tz	Q	R	Sh	Th	L	M	N

Each letter of a Word is substituted for that above or below it in the other line, thus forming a different word or making a cipher system. In the above instance, the word אחד (Achad = Unity) would become נצבת, a word the meaning of which I do not know (the example was taken at random) but which adds to 540. This number is that of another Word meaning "The Upper Part" or, it reduces to 9 (5+4+0 = 9) which is equal numerically to a word meaning "Became Powerful, Grew High." It may seem as if we had destroyed the Sacred Unity of our original Word in this instance, but again we may try the Tarot. The first letter of our word is ‫נ‬ = 50 = Tarot Key XIII. Now 13 is the numeration of the word AChD or Unity. This Trump is that of DEATH, which is called "The Child of the Great Transformers." Now the other letters ‫צת‬ by Tarot give THE STAR and THE UNIVERSE, so we may think this transformation indicates "THE DEATH of THE STAR UNIVERSE," but this is only apparent, for the UNITY cannot be destroyed, as we shall see on taking the Key of the whole word 540 = 5+4+0 = 9 = IX = THE HERMIT of the Tarot, carrying concealed beneath his cloak, his Lamp, in which Burns a STAR, thus secretly bringing the Light of Unity to the Adepts of the Inner College.

There are many other arrangements of the lower line of letters, but the name of the method employed is always obtained from the first two pairs of letters on the right hand end of the lines, thus in this case AN, BM.

Another method of Cipher Writing is called AIQ BKR or "The Qabalah of Nine Chambers" thus:

300	30	3	200	20	2	100	10	1
Sh	L	G	R	K	B	Q	I	A
600	60	6	500	50	5	400	40	4
M-final	S	V	K-final	N	H	Th	M	D
900	90	9	800	80	8	700	70	7
Tz-final	Tz	T	P-final	P	Ch	N-final	O	Z

By arranging the letters in groups of Units, Tens, and Hundreds, we obtain a system whereby a Dot placed in one of the Nine Chambers, would represent the Unit Letter, and Two Dots or Three Dots the Tens or Hundreds.

This grouping of the letters may be used in other ways, such as by taking the Tarot Cards Corresponding and thus obtaining new Combinations of ideas.

Those who are sufficiently versed in the Art of Q. B. L. sometimes draw inferences from the SHAPE of the Letters themselves, but this method is hardly for beginners. One well known example is the letter א (Aleph) which is said to symbolize the letter י (IVD) because it is formed of the letters י, ו, ד, which are those of Yod spelt in full. Or by another method, the letter כ (Kaph) might be said to conceal Yod, since Kaph = 20 and IVD = 20, etc.

Enough has been said to give the Student an idea of the best known Methods of the Literal Qabalah, and we may now pass on to a brief sketch of some of the important Qabalistic NUMBERS, by the study of which we shall obtain further Light on the Path.

CHAPTER EIGHT

Concerning Numbers, Symbols and Matters Cognate

The Three Interpretations of the Numbers from 1 to 10, given in "The Equinox" Volume I. Number 5, are so brief, concise and clear, that I am fain to depart from my intention to refrain from using books of reference and, with due acknowledgments to Fra. P.[1], quote the passages in full.

I

0. The Negative—the Infinite—the Circle, or the Point.

1. The Unity—the Positive—the Finite—the Line, derived from 0 by extension. The divine Being.

2. The Dyad—the Superfices, derived from 1 by reflection $\frac{1}{1}$ or by revolution of the line around its end. The Demiurge. The Divine Will.

3. The Triad, the Solid, derived from 1 and 2 by addition. Matter. The divine Intelligence.

4. The Quaternary, the solid existing in Time, matter as we know it. Derived from 2 by multiplication. The Divine Repose.

5. The Quinary, Force or Motion. The interplay of the divine Will with matter. Derived from 2 and 3 by addition.

6. The Senary, Mind. Derived from 2 and 3 by multiplication.

7. The Septenary, Desire. Derived from 3 and 4 by addition (There is however a secondary attribution of 7, making it the holiest and most perfect of the numbers).

8. The Ogdoad, Intellect (also Change in Stability). Derived from 2 and 3 by multiplication, $8 = 2^2$.

9. The Ennead, Stability in Change. Derived from 2 and 3 by multiplication, $9 = 3^3$.

(Note, all numbers divisible by nine are still so divisible, however the order of the figures is shifted.)

10. The Decad, the divine End. Represents 1 returning to 0. Derived from $1+2+3+4$.

11. The Hendecad, the accursed shells, that only exist without the divine Tree. $1+1 = 2$, in the evil sense of not being 1.

II

0. The Cosmic Egg.
1. The Self of Deity, beyond Fatherhood and Motherhood.
2. The Father.
3. The Mother.
4. The Father made flesh—authoritative and paternal.
5. The Mother made flesh—fierce and active.
6. The Son—partaking of all these natures.
7. The Mother degraded to mere animal emotion.
8. The Father degraded to mere animal reason.

9. The Son degraded to mere animal life.

10. The Daughter, fallen and touching with her hands the shells.

It will be noticed that this order represents creation as progressive degeneration—which we are compelled to think of as evil. In the human organism the same arrangement will be noticed.

III

0. The Pleroma of which our individuality is the monad: the "All-Self."

1. The Self—the divine Ego of which man is rarely conscious.

2. The Ego; that which thinks "I"—a falsehood, because to think "I" is to deny "not—I" and thus create the Dyad.

3. The Soul; since 3 reconciles 2 and 1, here are placed the aspirations to divinity. It is also the receptive as 2 is the assertive self.

4–9. The Intellectual Self, with its branches:

    4. Memory.

    5. Will.

    6. Imagination.

    7. Desire.

    8. Reason.

    9. Animal being.

6. The Conscious Self of the Normal Man; thinking itself free, and really the toy of its surroundings.

9. The Unconscious Self of the Normal Man. Reflex actions, circulation, breathing, digestion, etc., all pertain here.

10. The illusory physical envelope; the scaffolding of the building.

★★★★★★★★★★★★★

The above quotations will give the Student food for thought, and should be carefully studied in the light of what has been written in the previous chapters.

The study of the numbers above Ten involves a great deal of work, and far too lengthy an explanation for this brief treatise. In the SEPHER SEPHIROTH (to be found in "The Equinox" Vol. I, Number 8),[2] we have a more or less complete Qabalistic Dictionary of Numbers and their corresponding Words. This book is quite invaluable. The Student, as time goes on and he advances upon the Path, finds CERTAIN NUMBERS are of peculiar importance to him, and these become so closely associated with his Work, that they form Keys to the innermost recesses of his being. These will not always be the same for each student, rather each must discover his own, sometimes by years of toil. The writer has found the Numbers 0, 1, 13, 31, 86, 93, 111, 136, 141, 165, 300, 418, 419, 496, 620, 777, 913, 963, all very closely associated with his Work, besides, in a more general way, such great Numbers as 65, 78, 156, 666, etc.

It is not within the scope of this work to discuss the many wonderful things that have arisen in connection with the above Numbers, as far as the author is concerned, but in order to give the Student some idea of the Nature of the Sepher Sepiroth, and how words may be connected through their numerical value, I will take 31 numbers and their equivalents as an example. The first 24 of these numbers have been chosen simply on account of their close juxtaposition on the

TREE of LIFE. The others, being of the Grand Scale, are interesting on that account. I commence with 12, since 1 and 2 are Kether and Chokmah, then 13, as 1 and 3=Kether and Binah, and so on.

12

He longed for, missed	אוה
He departed, went forth	אזר
A little book, pamphlet, letter; tools	גט
To multiply	דגה
A City of Edom	הבה
HE. (ה Is referred to Mater, ו to Pater, א to Corona)	הוא
Vau; hook, nail, pin	וו
This, that	זה
To penetrate, be sharp; (Ch.) one	חד

13

A small bundle, bunch	אגדה
Beloved. Love	אהבה
Unity	אחד
Hated	איב
Emptiness	בהו
Raised up	גהה
Chokmah, 42-fold Name in Yetzirah (See 777)	גי
Anxiety	דאגה
A Fisher	דוג
Thunder; to meditate; he removed	הגה
A city of Edom	הדר
Here; this	וז

A locust   חגב
He shall come   יבא

16

Hyssopus   אזוב
He seized, cleaved to   אחז
Elevated, exalted, high   גבוה
(Verb. subst.) Injury, war, lust; fell   הוה
She   היא
Alas!—Woe   וי
Like, equal to   זוג

21

Existence, Being, the Kether-name of GOD   אהיה
But, yet, certainly   אך
Deep meditation   הגיג
Ah!—Alas!   הוי
Purity, innocence   זהו
Vide Sepher Yetzirah   יהו

23

Parted, removed, separated   זחח
Joy   חדוה
A thread   חוט
Life   חיה

24

He whom I love   אהובי
He who loves me   אוהבי
A Mercurial GOD. His essence is אז, 8   אזבוגה

Substance; a body גויה
A pauper דך
Angel of 2 C.[3] הבביה
Abundance זיז
A water-pot, a large earthen vessel כד

26

The Numbers of the Sephiroth of the
Middle Pillar; 1+6+9+10
[Vide K.D. L.C.K. p. 273][4] הויה
Seeing, looking at חזה
Sight, vision חזוה
TETRAGRAMMATON, "Jehovah" יהוה
the Unutterable Name, the Lost Word
Kebad, husband of the impure Lilith כבד
[K.D. L.C.K. 464]

31

How? איך
GOD of Chesed, and of Kether of Briah אל
To go הוך
A beating, striking, collision הכאה
And there was. [Vide S.D.I. par. 31][5] ויהי
K. of S. Fig. 31[6] ייאי
Not לא

32

Coalescence of אהיה and יהוה Macroprosopus אהיהוה
and Microprosopus. This is symbolized by the
Hexagram. Suppose the 3 ה's conceal the 3
Mothers א, מ, ש and we get 358 q. v.

Lord	בל
Angel of 5 W.[7]	והויה
Copula Maritalis	זיווג
Was pure	זכה
Zig-zag, fork-lighting	חזיז
Unity K.D. L.C.K. p. 432	יחיד
Glory	כבוד
Mind, heart	לב

35

Agla, a name of GOD; notariqon of Ateh Gibor le–Olahm Adonai	אגלא
Boundary limit	גבל
He will go	יהך

45

Intelligence of ♄	אגיאל
Adam	אדם
The Fool	אמד
Redemption, liberation	גאולה
To grow warm	חם
Heaven of Tiphereth	זבול
Hesitated. [Vide no. 405]	זחל
Spirit of ♄	זזאל
She who ruins	חבלה
Tet. in Yetzirah	יוד הא ואו הא
Greatly, strongly	מאד
Yetzirah's 'Secret Nature' [Vide I.R.Q. xxxiv.]	מה

46

A name of GOD	אלהי
A female slave; cubitus	אמה
Tin, the metal of ♃	בדיל
A dividing, sundering, separation	הבדלה
Angel of 7 S.	הההאל
A ruiner	חובל
Angel ruling ♉	טואל
Levi, Levite	לוי

47

Foolish, silly. (Stultus)	אויל
A weeping	בכייה
Cloud; high place; waves; fortress	במה
Angel ruling ♍	יואל
To clutch, hold	חלט

54

A basin, bowl, vessel. [Ex. xxiv. 6]	אגן
Rest	דמי
A Tribe of Israel; to judge, rule. [Vide K.D. L.C.K. p. 37]	דן
Pertaining to summer	חום
My flame; enchantments	להטי
A bed; stick, rod	מטה
To remove	נד

56

Dread, terror	אימה
He suffered	אנה

Angel of 4 C.   הייאל
Day   יום
Beautiful   נאה

58

[Vide no. 499]   אהבים
[Vide K.D. L.C.K. p. 69] An ear   אזן
Night Demon of 1st Dec. ♐   דאגן
My strength, power, might   חילי
Love, kindness, grace; notariqon of Chokmah   חן
     Nesethrah, the Secret Wisdom
Ruler of Water   טליהד
Angel of 6 S.   ייזאל
Angel of 3 P.   להחיה
[Vide K.D. L.C.K. p. 69]   נח

67

[Vide K.D. L.C.K. p. 57]   אוני
The Understanding   בינה
Night Demon of 3rd Dec. II   וינא
Zayin   זין
Debased   זלל
To embalm   חנט
Angel of 3C.   יבמיה

69

A manger, stable; an enclosure   אבום
Myrtle   הדם
L.A. Angel of ♓   וכביאל

78

There are 78 cards in the Tarot. Σ (1—12).
  The Mystic Number of Kether as Hua.
  The sum of the Key-Numbers of the
  Supernal Beard.
Angel of 10 W.   אומאל
Angel of Ra Hoor Khuit   איואם
Briatic Palace of Chesed   היכל אהבה
Angel of ♂   זמאל
The breaker, dream   חלם
To pity   חמל
To initiate   חנך
Angel of 2 S.   יזלאל
Angel of 1st Dec. ♉   כדמדי
Bread (P's. lxxviii. 25) = חלם, by metathesis.   לחם
  [K.D. L.C.K. p. 500]
Angel of 2 S.   מבהאל
The Influence from Kether   מזלא
Salt   מלח
The name of a Giant   עזא

79

Boaz, one of the Pillars of the Temple of Solomon   בעז
Die   גוע
Angel of 8 S.   ומבאל
Jachin, one of the Pillars of the Temple   יאחין
  of Solomon
3rd ♄   סיט
Conjunction, meeting, union   עדה

[Vide K.D. L.C.K. p. 114]	אלון
A cup	אסוך
Angel of 1st Dec.15 ♓[8]	בהלמי
Blasphemed	גדף
Standards, military ensigns	דגלים
Determined	זמם
White Storks	חסידה
Whiteness; frankincense; Sphere of ☾	לבנה

Shut up	גוף
Body	גוף
Silence	דממה
Angel of 9 S.[9]	מחיאל

Σ (1—13). The Mystic Number of Kether as Achad.　　91
　　　The Number of Paths in the Supernal Beard;
　　　according to the number of the Letters, כ = 11, etc.

A tree	אילן
Amen. [Cf 741]	אמן
The Ephod	אפוד
The "יהוה אדני", interlaced	יאהדונהי
Angel of 4 S.[10]	כליאל
Archangel of Geburah	כמאל
Food, fare	מאכל
Angel	מלאך
Daughter, virgin, bride, Kore	מלכא
Manna	מנא
A hut, tent	סוכה
Pekht, 'extension'	פאהה

111

Red. [Vide Gen. xxv. 25]	אדמונא
A name of GOD	אחד הוא אלהים
A thousand; Aleph	אלף
Ruin, destruction, sudden death	אסן
AUM	אעם
Thick darkness	אפל
Passwords of . . .	יוד יהוה אדני
Mad	מהולל
Angel of ☉	נכיאל
Common holocaust; an ascent	עולה
A Duke of Edom	עלוה
Title of Kether. (Mirum occultum)	פלא

222

Urias	אוריה
"Unto the Place." [Ex. xxiii. 20]	אל המקום
Whiteness	הוורה
Goodly mountain. [Ex. ill. 25]	הר טוב
Now, already; K'bar, "the river Khebar"; Day Demon of 3rd Dec.	כבר
I will chase	ראויה

333

Qabalah of the Nine Chambers	איק בכר
Choronzon. [Vide Dr Dee, & Lib. 418, 10th Aire][11]	חורונזון
Snow	שלג

	444
The Sanctuary	מקדש
Damascus	דמשק

	555
Obscurity	עפתה

Σ (1—36). ☉. The Number of   666
     THE BEAST.

Aleister E. Crowley	אלהיסטהר ה כרעולהי
Aleister Crowley	
[Rabbi Battiscomber Gunn's v.1.]	אליסטיר קרולי
The number 5, which is 6 (הא),	הא x אלף
on the Grand Scale	
Qliphoth of ♓	נשימירו
Spirit of ☉	סורת
Ommo Satan, the 'Evil Triad' of	עממו סתן
Satan-Typhon, Apophras, and Besz	
The Name Jesus	שם יהשוה

	777

The Flaming Sword, if the path from Binah to	
Chesed be taken as = 3. For ג connects Arikh	
Anpin with Zauir Anpin. One is the Ruach	
of the Elohim of Lives	אחת רוח אלהים חיים
The World of Shells	עולם הקליפות

The foregoing will give the Student some little material to work upon, and to experiment with, in tracing out some of the correspondences for himself, though he needs "The Sepher Sephiroth" for reference and further research. Also he will find "The Essay on Number" in "The Temple of Solomon the King," Equinox Vol. I, Number 5, and "A Note on Genesis," Equinox Volume I, Number 2, of tremendous help and value.

We may now give an example of the way in which we may use the TAROT SYMBOLS for the interpretation of certain WORDS. The relation of these Symbols to the Letters of the Hebrew Alphabet, each spelt in full, has been ably shown in one of the articles mentioned above, but I do not know that any attempt has been made to interpret the Names of the 10 Sephiroth in a similar manner. The Symbolism of the Tarot Trumps being Universal, many interpretations could be given representing different planes. Here is one, which came to me yesterday which if deeply MEDITATED upon, may prove illuminating.

AN ATTEMPT TO INTERPRET THE NAMES OF THE SEPHIROTH FROM MALKUTH TO KETHER BY TAROT Fra∴ א June 12, 1922, E.V.

10. Malkuth.   מלכות. The REDEEMER of the BALANCE of the FORCES OF LIFE is the HIEROPHANT of the UNIVERSE.

9. Yesod.   יסוד. The SECRET of TEMPERANCE shown by the HIEROPHANT to the EMPRESS.

8. Hod.   הוד. The EMPEROR through the HIEROPHANT finds LOVE (The Empress).

7. Netzach.   נצח. Transformation through DEATH awaits the STAR in the CHARIOT.

6. Tiphereth.   תפארת. The UNIVERSAL TOWER is Blasted by the FOLLY of the SUN of the UNIVERSE.

5. Geburah.   גבורה. The HOLY LAW of MAGICK as taught by the HIEROPHANT of the SUN is applied by the EMPEROR.

4. Chesed.   חסד. The CHARIOT of TEMPERATE-LOVE.

3. Binah.   בינה. The MAGICAL SECRET of DEATH transforms the EMPEROR.

2. Chokmah.   חכמה. The CHARIOT (or Balanced Control) of the LIFE FORCES, REDEEMS the EMPEROR.

1. Kether.   כתר. In the "Hollow of the Hand" (כ) of the LORD OF THE FORCES OF LIFE is the UNIVERSAL SUN.

The Student should take his Tarot Cards and study them very carefully in connection with the above, and it may be well if he try to obtain other interpretations, say in the order from Kether to Malkuth, representing the Descent of the Light from above.

He should also study the Shape and Parts of the "Tree of Life" itself, and he will notice that the whole forms an ANKH or Egyptian Key of Life, which is again the symbol of Venus (♀). It should be noticed how the "Tree" forms Three Pillars, those of Mercy and Severity, with the Pillar of Mildness between them. Again, the Hexagram is formed by the Upper

Six Sephiroth, and the lines of the Pentagram may be drawn by connecting the upper Five. The "Tree" can be divided into Seven Planes, etc., etc. In fact, one cannot exhaust the possibilities of its study.

I should like to remark once again, however, that this is, after all, just a CONVENIENT MEANS OF CLASSIFI-CATION. Sometimes we desire to Symbolize ALL as Unity, and we should probably use merely a Circle or Point. Again, there is the DUAL Aspect. Then the Great THREE-FOLD DIVISION as the TRINITY. Then the FOUR-FOLD nature of the ELEMENTS can be expressed as a SQUARE or CROSS. But once we use the CROSS, there is the POINT OF INTERSECTION indicating the Hidden SPIRIT, so we adopt the Great FIVE-FOLD classification of THE PENTAGRAM, Symbol of THE MICROCOSM, MAN. Again we wish to symbolize our correspondence to the MACROCOSM and we use the HEXAGRAM, or SIX-FOLD STAR, upon which we place the Planetary Symbols and the Holy Seven-fold Name ARARITA, for this Star has a CENTRE which is attributed to The SUN and this makes it also a SEVEN-FOLD means of classification. Next comes our TEN-FOLD QABALISTIC TREE of LIFE, with all its possibilities of extension through the 22 paths, 4 Worlds, etc. and its TAROT ATTRIBUTIONS. These, again, can just as well be expressed in the form of a Great Wheel, with the TWELVE SIGNS of the ZODIAC on its rim, and it is from the Rulers of the Decanates that the Divinatory meanings of the Small Cards are obtained. Lastly, since this Wheel has a CENTRE it expresses THIRTEEN, and we may arrange our Zodiacal attributions on a GREEK CROSS of THIR-

TEEN SQUARES with SPIRIT at the CENTRE. So, you see, you must not think the Plans are fixed, they can always be interchanged, according to the Nature of that aspect we most desire to make prominent.

But remember, in all this diversity, is the One underlying UNITY, which itself arose from that which is NOT.

CHAPTER NINE

Of That Which Was and Is and Shall Be

"The word of Sin is Restriction"

"Love is the law, love under will"

"Do what thou wilt shall be the whole of the Law!"[1]

These words may sound strangely in your ears who hear them for the first time; and what have they to do with the Qabalah and the Tree of Life?

This little treatise would not be complete without some mention of the wonderful Qabalistic correspondences to be found in LIBER LEGIS, The Book of the Law of the Aeon of Horus.

You may never have heard of this Book, yet since it is written therein "The Law is for all,"[2] it is well that I should give you a brief glimpse of this matter. In order to do so, I shall be obliged to make some explanation as to how I came to apply myself to the study of its manifold Mysteries, which have gradually been unfolded in such a marvelous manner.

On March 21st, 1904 E..V. occurred, what is known to
the adepts as, THE EQUINOX OF THE GODS, that is to
say, the advent of a New Aeon, and a consequent change of
Office in the Great Hierarchy which is engaged in the
Initiation of Humanity on this planet. The Old Order
changeth and all things become New. About this time, under
very extraordinary circumstances, Frater O. M. an Adept of
the A∴A∴ received a communication through, what appears
to have been, a praeterhuman Channel. This communication is known as LIBER AL vel LEGIS, and consists of 220
verses, divided into Three Chapters. The 1st chapter contains instructions from NUIT, Lady of the Starry Heavens,
the 2nd from HADIT, the inmost essential Self of All, and
the 3rd from Ra-Hoor-Khuit, Lord of the Aeon. The full
details of this communication, will be given to the world in
the proper manner, time, and place and by the proper
Authority.

In 1909, I—Achad—-became a Probationer of the Great
Brotherhood known as the A∴A∴, and for some years I
toiled at the Great Work, first under the guidance of one Fra
∴ P.A.[3] and later under Fra ∴ O. M.[4] Thus did I first contact this New Current. In 1916, at the Summer Solstice, I
underwent a Great Initiation, which showed in a certain way
I was destined to fulfil one of the prophesies in Liber Legis
in a most unusual and unlooked-for manner. This was followed, 18 months later at the Winter Solstice 1917 E.V., by
a continuation of the Great Initiation on another Plane. The
first dealt with the SEPHIROTH and the second with the
PATHS of the Tree of Life. Both led to an extraordinary
Unification of the Whole Tree in my consciousness. The

Initiation of 1917 (and by this I do not mean of the "Lodge Room" kind, but one directed entirely by the Masters of Wisdom from other Planes of Being), resulted, about a year later, when time had enabled me to get a clear perspective of the event, in my obtaining a certain Qabalistic Key to Liber Legis (as prophesied therein), and this Key was delivered to Frater O. M., who had by then become The Master Therion. This was the means of opening many of the doors of the Palace, and was accepted as sufficient proof that I had certain Work to do in connection with "Liber Legis" and the New Aeon. For myself, how could I doubt or avoid it, even if I would? I had aspired to the Highest, and this was the result of my aspiration, this close tie with events, which time will show to be of unimaginable importance to all Humanity. In "Liber Legis" there is much which is entirely strange, and at first repugnant, For five years Frater O. M., who received it, endeavoured to avoid His task of proclaiming the Law to All, yet such depths of Wisdom were hidden in this Book, such wonderful fore-knowledge of events, that it PROVED itself to be unavoidable. It is not my work to comment on this Book,—that has been wisely provided for in the Book itself,—but I do wish to point out that the Qabalistic implications are simply marvelous, both in regard to the depths of the concealed meanings, and the simplicity of the Cipher when they are brought to Light. Such statements as "Nothing is a secret key of this law. Sixty-one the Jews call it; I call it eight, eighty, four hundred and eighteen. But they have the half: unite by thine art so that all disappear," become perfectly clear and lucid once the Key is found. And this is but one of its characteristic Qabalistic puzzles.

I point this out to show how my little study of the Holy Qabalah, proved of such great help when the time came and I needed to make use of it. I may remark that the Poise and Equilibrium which it gave me, proved my salvation time and again in the most terrible Ordeals, keeping my inner Being balanced and calm amidst a malestrom of conflicting forces, and enabling me to co-ordinate them into an orderly Whole. Finally, it has led me to, what I believe is, the reconstruction of the Original Qabalistic Plan. It explains the Path indicated by the Child Horus in the First AETHYR of "The Vision and the Voice" obtained by Frater O. M. in 1909 E. V. I am dealing with these things in the Appendix to this little Book. How could I have guessed what the writing of it would lead to? I started with the idea of giving my Students an outline of the System I had been using for years, the system whereby I was led to Attain, by which—as has been amply proved—Attainment is possible. Yet, suddenly, without effort, I am led to discover, what appears to be a far simpler Road; on the same Tree, 'tis true, but by different Paths. A Road, the possibilities of which are yet to be discovered, but which may help Humanity to regain the Crown more easily than of yore. A System fulfilling the prophesies of the OLD as well as those of the NEW Aeon, as it is written in Liber Legis: "All words are sacred and all prophets true; save only that they understand a little."[5]

Those who have faithfully endeavoured to live up to the instruction "Do what thou wilt shall be the whole of the Law!," have indeed found this to be the "Straight and Narrow Way." This means that we must discover, each for himself, the Will of God, the Creative Word, in the Depths of our own Being. By finding our True Purpose, and fulfilling it, and it alone—leaving others the Freedom to find and fulfil theirs—we live in Harmony with the Universal Will and Movement of Things, as Stars in the Body of Nuit, the Mother of Heaven.

As we follow this Way, we find our lives corresponding more closely with the Universal Life; we notice the Great Cyclic Laws operative in us, as in all else. Events begin to occur, which check up with Astrological conditions, we find ourselves more and more at one with Nature and Nature's Forces. Our Inner Being gives us LIGHT whereever we travel, and day by day we get closer to the Central Mystery of Being till we can truly exclaim "I and My Father are One." These are some of the things that the New Law has taught me, and for which I can never be too thankful to Him who proclaimed it.

There is no fixity and sameness in this Law. Each has a certain Purpose, a certain part to play in the Cosmic Drama. No two Wills are alike, let us see to it that we never again foolishly try to break the Will of another. The Beauty of Creation may only be understood through its great diversity. Never by trying to make all men express one set pattern or Ideal, can the Plan of Creation be realized. Nature insures Individual Freedom through Order; remember that. This Law does not lead to disorder and confusion, but to the only true Order, wherein each Unit, working according to the True Will of the Whole, makes his individual Work an expression of Himself as an unique part of that Whole. WILL is that which produces CHANGE which is LIFE. Stagnation or fixity, is DEATH. Therefore fear not CHANGE, but embrace it with open arms, for all change is of the nature of LOVE, which is the tendency of any two things to become ONE thus losing themselves in the process. We must learn to rid ourselves of the Illusionary idea of the little "self" as something distinct and separate from the Great Life around us. We must unite ourselves, through LOVE, with Larger and Grander conceptions, thus building up for ourselves that "House not made with Hands, eternal in the Heavens." But do we really build this? In a certain measure, yes, for it requires our Willing co-operation. But the Complete Temple is potentially inherent in the Substance of our own Being, and the Great Architect is in Every Temple Shrine, for He indeed is the Master Builder, and He Builds from within OUT-WARDS. Thus we expand into the Body of our Lady Nuit, even as She contracteth and holdeth all the parts of our Temple firmly together.

CHAPTER TEN

Of the Kingdom and of the Bride

The last chapter may have appeared rather like a digression from our main Treatise, but it may also prove a Door leading us to discover the Closed Palaces of The King and Queen.

I have little more to add to what I have already outlined in the earlier Chapters of this Book, for I feel that I have placed in the hands of true Students that which will enable them to obtain a grasp of the fundamental ideas of the Qabalah, without overloading them with details, which can be taken up later at the pleasure of the enquirer.

The "Path" is a long one, whichever way we travel; some say that it goes on forever so that "Only those are happy who desire the unobtainable." But Yesterday, To-day and Forever are all included in the HERE and NOW. At least, even in normal consciousness, the Past is Past and we are the result of it. The Future, being determined by the PRESENT, let us act rightly NOW, and that will take care of itself.

If we would obtain the Fruits of the Tree of Life, we must be prepared to put in a little of this Present Time on the study of First Principles. When we have a grasp of these the rest will come in due course, for, as I explained before, The Hidden Influence FLOWS easily once the channels have been opened up.

Now a few further words in regard to the "Channels of Mezla" or "Paths" of the Tree of Life. I have hinted at another possible arrangement of these "Paths" for it is said "When the Great Serpent raised his Head unto Daäth (Knowledge, the Child of Chokmah and Binah) his Head was BLASTED, therefore is all knowledge piece-meal." We obtain a hint from the earliest Qabalistic Treatise "The Sepher Yetzirah" or "Book of Formations" for it says "Ten are the numbers of the ineffable Sephiroth, ten and not nine, ten and not eleven. Learn this wisdom and be wise in the understanding of it, investigate these numbers, and draw knowledge from them, FIX THE DESIGN IN ITS PURITY, and pass from it to its creator seated on his throne" again Rittangelius[1] gives "REPLACE THE FORMATIVE POWER UPON HIS THRONE" and Postellus[2] states "RESTORE THE DEVICE OR WORKMANSHIP TO ITS PLACE."

So we see there appears to have been some mystery to be cleared up in order to restore the Temple of the Qabalah to its true Splendour.

Now let me give you a few hints from "Liber Legis."

Chapter I, Verse 49 reads "Abrogate are all rituals, all ordeals all words and signs. Ra-Hoor Khuit hath taken his seat in the East at the Equinox of the Gods; and let Asar be with Isa, who also are one. But they are not of me. Let Asar be the adorant, Isa, the sufferer; Hoor in his secret name and splendour is the Lord initiating."

50. There is a word to say about the Hierophantic task. Behold! there are three ordeals in one, and it may be given in three ways. The gross must pass through fire; let the fine be tried in intellect, and the lofty chosen ones in the highest; Thus ye have star & star, system & system; let not one know well the other." These are the words of Nuit, Lady of the Starry Heavens. Again She speaks in verse 57 ★ ★ ★ "All these old letters of my book are aright; but ϡ is not the Star. This also is secret: my prophet shall reveal it to the wise." The "old book," is of course The Book of Hermes or Tarot. The prophet did explain this change in His comment to Liber Legis.

Again Hadit speaks in Chapter II, Verse 2.

"Come! all ye, and learn the secret that hath not yet been revealed. I, Hadit am the complement of Nu, my bride. I am not extended, and Khabs (meaning a Star) is the name of my House.

3. In the sphere I am everywhere the centre, as she, the circumference is nowhere found.

4. Yet she shall be known and I never.

5. Behold! the rituals of old time are black. Let the evil ones be cast away; let the good ones be purged by the prophet! Then shall this Knowledge go aright."

And again Verse 34.

"But ye, o my people, rise up & awake!

35. Let the rituals be rightly performed with joy & beauty!" All this seems to point to a new order of things that will regenerate this Kingdom so that the Will of the Highest may be done on Earth as it is done in Heaven. But how shall this be brought about? How shall Malkuth the Daughter, be

Raised to the Throne of the Mother and at last come to understand?

It was prophesied through Frater O. M. in the "Vision and the Voice" 8th Aethyr. "UNTO HIM THAT UNDER-STANDETH AT LAST do I deliver the secrets of truth in such wise that the least of the little children of the light may run to the knees of the mother and be brought to understand."

So we need have no fear, the way is to be made plain, for one has understood at last.

Therefore in the Words of Horus the Crowned Child of the Aeon (First Aethyr) will I point out the Way, for it is written:

"Thou shalt laugh at the folly of the fool. Thou shalt learn the wisdom of the wise. And thou shalt be initiate in holy things. And thou shalt be learned in the things of Love. And thou shalt be mighty in the things of war. And thou shalt interpret the oracles. And thou shalt drive all these before thee in thy car, and though by none of these canst thou reach up to me, yet by each of these must thou attain to me. And thou must have the strength of the lion, and the secrecy of the hermit. And thou must turn the wheel of life. And thou must hold the balances of Truth. Thou must pass through the great Waters a Redeemer. Thou must have the tail of the Scorpion, and the poisoned arrows of the Archer, and the dreadful horns of the Goat. And so shall thou break down the fortress that guardeth the Palace of the King my son. And thou must work by the light of the Star and of the Moon and of the Sun, and by the dreadful light of judgment that is the birth of the Holy Spirit within thee. When these shall have destroyed the universe, then mayest thou enter the palace of the Queen my daughter."[3]

Thus, gentle readers, are we shown the Way to the Palace of the Bride.

Set ye out upon that "Never-ending journey, each step of which is an unutterable reward" and ye shall have naught to complain of, at

THE BRIDE'S RECEPTION.

June 13th, 1922.

APPENDICES TO

Q. B. L.

OR

THE BRIDE'S RECEPTION

Note

This Appendix has purposely been left in the form of Notes, made by the Author as certain new aspects of the Qabalah were revealed to him. No attempt has been made to put these into good literary form or to draw together all the various conclusions into a complete Whole. The Student will find it necessary to use minute care in tracing out the different Paths indicated, and it may be well to adopt the advice of Chuang Tzu, as translated by Giles:

"Have no established mental criteria, and thus see all things as ONE."

APPENDIX TO CHAPTER TWO

Concerning the Natural Basis of Correspondences in the Hebrew Alphabet

It has been intimated to the Author that some Qabalists consider the Symbolic Names of the Hebrew Letters, taken in their natural order, conceal a description of the Creative Process or natural Cycle of Generation. I have never seen this written of, but one might perhaps attempt to verify the notion and see if it has any foundation in truth.

א	The Ox.	The Male Generative Power of the Father.
ב	The House.	That which shelters. The Womb of the Mother.
ג	The Camel.	One who carries Water in its belly, therefore suggests that the Mother is with Child by the Father and that it floats in the amniotic fluid.
ד	The Door.	Means of ingress and egress whereby the Child makes its entrance into the World.

ה	The Window.	Lets in Light from outside, suggests that the Child is brought to light.
ו	The Nail.	That which unites or joins. The Umbilical Cord.
ז	The Sword.	That which severs the cord.
ח	The Fence.	Suggests an outside enclosure around the field or garden of the Father (Ox) viz: the child lives within its parents' estates until—
ט	The Serpent.	The sex-force awakes at Puberty.
י	The hand.	A natural symbol after recognition of sexual desire.
כ	The Palm.	(of hand). Obvious from last symbol.
ל	The Ox-goad.	Desire goads him on towards the opposite sex.
מ	Water.	The Symbol of the Feminine.
נ	Fish.	Seed.
ס	Prop.	Erection.
ע	Eye.	Sees object of desire.
פ	Mouth.	Expresses desire by kiss.
צ	Fish-hook.	That which wishes to draw forth fish. Desire aroused in mate.
ק	Back of Head.	Suggests one lying on back of head.

ר	Head.	Suggests another head, countenance beholds counterance.
ש	Tooth.	Suggests "to bite." Woman crushes Serpent's head.
ת	Tau.	Egyptian Tau-cross. Instrument used to measure the depth of water in the Nile. Phallus in extension.

Thus we see the Cycle complete. The Son acts as his Father—Aleph—did before him, the Daughter becomes the Mother. As it was in the Beginning, is now, and ever shall be. AMN.

The above is capable of development along other and slightly different lines, according to the grade to which the student belongs, and the aspect of the process to be symbolized. I have suggested the purely physical, since it would be a very natural one with the primitive peoples. The scheme is possible of interpretation on other planes, no doubt, but I have kept entirely to the Symbolic titles of the letters without using, for instance, their Yetziratic or Tarot Correspondences.

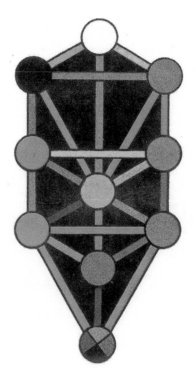

Plate 1—The Minutum Mundum.

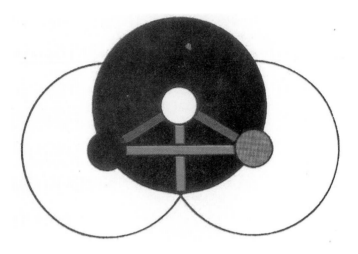

Plate 2—The Supernal Triad.

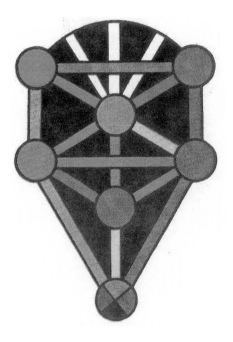

Plate 3—The Second Order.

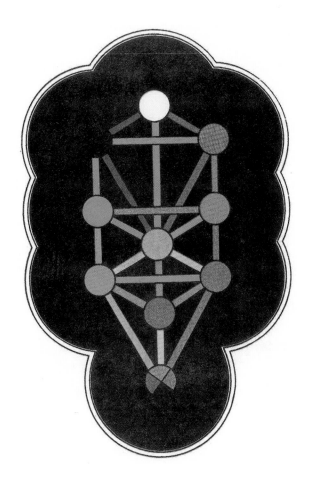

Plate 4—The Third Order.

APPENDIX TO
CHAPTERS THREE AND FOUR

Concerning the Twenty-Two Paths and the Attributions of the Tarot Trumps

Section I

Having written as far as the end of the brief description of the XVIIth Trump called THE STAR, I noticed the time and finding it already the small hours of the morning of May 31st E.V., I rested a moment from my labours on this my little book. My mind went back to the words I had just written and underscored, "The symbolism of the **Paths** is more important when considered from the BOTTOM TO THE TOP OF THE TREE." I went to bed, being right weary, but this thought kept recurring to me until, of a sudden, a glimmer of its tremendous importance illuminated my Understanding. I began mentally working on a plan which had never before been hinted at by any of the so-called Authorities. It seemed to have great possibilities, but I slept upon it and began further investigations in the morning.

The results of these investigations, which have been in progress until this morning, (June 2nd, 1922 E.V.) have proved so far reaching in their consequences that I have found it difficult to decide as to the best manner of dealing with this discovery, which at first sight seems to revolutionize the whole System.

I have decided, therefore, to present to you—and here I do not alone refer to new students but to ALL those of whatever Grade who have based their System of Attainment on the TREE OF LIFE—the first ideas of this revelation, but without dealing with the complexities which will occur to those who realize the consequences involved in making the further adjustments which appear to be indicated, or my own attempts to solve these problems.

This explanation will involve a matter which had not been fully discussed in the previous pages, viz:—

The Sword and the Serpent

The Qabalists tell us that the SEPHIROTH were emanated by means of the FLAMING SWORD, or LIGHTNING FLASH, which descended from Kether unto Malkuth (as shown in the diagram Chapter One.) They also say that this was followed by the ASCENT of the SERPENT of WISDOM who thus formed the PATHS. They showed his head at the top of the Tree, in the path leading from Kether to Chokmah, which is in turn the First Path of the FLAMING SWORD.

All the known authorities have then continued to number the remaining 22 of the 32 Paths of Wisdom, from Path 11 (joining Kether and Chokmah) to Path 32 (joining Yesod and Malkuth). Students have only to refer to such well known Authorities as Mr. W. Wynn Westcott, in his Introduction to the Study of the Kabalah (Watkins 1910), Book 777 (London

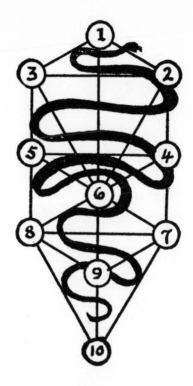

Fig. 10

1909), THE EQUINOX, Volume I, Number 2, which shows the attributions of Mr. Mathers and the Golden Dawn, etc., to prove this assertion to be a recognized fact. One may now question how it was that the SERPENT who formed the Paths by ASCENDING The Tree, could possibly have started at the Top, and why previous commentators have never taken this vital idea into consideration.

Anyway, let us find out what would happen if we followed the SERPENT of WISDOM (נחש = 358), which the Qabalists attributed to the Messiah (משיח = 358), and, remembering that "The Wisdom of God is Foolishness with Men," start on our upward journey by the ELEVENTH Path leading from MALKUTH to YESOD and attributed to the Tarot Trump marked 0 = THE FOOL.

We shall then find by following exactly the Reverse Order of the Paths as they were numbered, keeping exactly to the Order of the Letters from Aleph to Tau, and adopting (provisionally) the attributions of the Elements, Planets and Zodiac, exactly as previously shown, that the Tree will take on the following aspect.

The ELEVENTH Path from Malkuth to Yesod, attributed to AIR, will be Aleph, = The Fool, = AIR.

The TWELFTH Path from Malkuth to Hod (the Sphere of MERCURY) will be Beth, the Magician = MERCURY (Note his four elemental weapons coming from Malkuth, the Sphere of the Elements).

The THIRTEENTH Path from YESOD (The Sphere of the MOON) to Hod, will be the High Priestess = Gimmel = The MOON. (Note she holds the TORA or TARO on her lap and has the Moon under her feet.)

The FOURTEENTH Path from Malkuth to Netzach (the Sphere of VENUS) will be The Empress = Daleth = VENUS.

The FIFTEENTH Path from Yesod to Netzach will be The Emperor, (Consort of The Empress) = Hé = Aries. (Second Decan of Aries is Ruled by Venus according to Egyptian Astrology, though I am only provisionally content in regard to this Path.)

The SIXTEENTH Path from Hod to Netzach (the Sphere of VENUS) is the Hierophant = Vau = Taurus which is RULED by VENUS. (Note this position of the Hierophant in the centre of the Veil between the First and Second Orders.)

The SEVENTEENTH Path from Hod (the Sphere of MERCURY) to Tiphereth is the Lovers = Zain = Gemini which is RULED by MERCURY. (Note the Sun above their heads on card.)

The EIGHTEENTH Path from Yesod (the Sphere of the MOON) to Tiphereth is the Chariot = ‏ח‎ = Cheth = Cancer which is RULED by the MOON. (Initiates will note the symbolism of this Card of the New Aeon uniting with that of The Hierophant, and how he has harnessed the Black and White Sphinxes, etc.)

The NINETEENTH Path from Netzach to Tiphereth (the Sphere of the SUN) is Strength = Teth = Leo which is RULED by the SUN. (Note the Lion of the Sun or Leo and the Woman of Venus = Netzach.)

The TWENTIETH Path from Hod (the Sphere of MERCURY) to Geburah is THE HERMIT = Yod = VIRGO, the other sign (Besides Gemini) which is RULED by MERCURY.

The TWENTY-FIRST Path from Tiphereth to Geburah (the Sphere of MARS) is The Wheel of Fortune = ‏כ‎ = Kaph = Jupiter. (Here we find something which does not seem to follow this wonderful plan of the Planetary Paths meeting their OWN SEPHIROTH and in this one instance I am going to indicate the nature of a change which might make a great deal of difference to the rest of our plan. There appears no valid reason why ‏כ‎, Kaph should be attributed to Jupiter and ‏פ‎, Pé to Mars. The letters are very similar in appearance, except that Pé has an additional TONGUE and means The MOUTH, while Kaph is THE PALM of THE HAND. On the other hand Jupiter is the Sphere of Authority from whence comes the Instructions for the Order and might be Pé, The Mouth, while Mars, (with its New Aeon implicits as the Lord of SILENCE and of STRENGTH) is perhaps better symbolized by the PALM of the HAND (which is empty) i. e. KAPH.

Making this provisional change we should find the TWENTY-FIRST Path from Tiphereth to Geburah (the Sphere of MARS) is the Blasted Tower = Kaph = MARS. (Also note that the "Palm of the hand" is adjacent to the Path of Yod = The Hand.)

The TWENTY-SECOND Path from Netzach (the Sphere of VENUS) to Chesed is Justice = Lamed = Libra which is RULED by VENUS.

The TWENTY-THIRD Path from Tiphereth to Chesed would be the Hanged-Man = Mem = WATER, and Chesed is attributed to WATER.

The TWENTY-FOURTH Path from Geburah (the Sphere of MARS) to Chesed, is Death = Nun = Scorpio RULED by MARS. Note that this forms the Second Reciprocal Path or VEIL OF THE ABYSS above which IDEAS ARE ONLY TRUE INSOFAR AS THEY CONTAIN THEIR OWN OPPOSITES.

PAST THIS VEIL I do not feel permitted to lead you at this time. You may trace up the correspondences for yourselves and will find that in some instances, according to the accepted order of things, there will be difficulties in making perfect adjustments. One will also discover some startling symbolism, such as the conjunction of the Sun and Moon, of the Letters O. and N. etc., but the whole matter is of such importance that I can make no attempt to disclose my further surmises. Enough has been said to establish the possibility of a PERFECT SYSTEM of CORRESPONDENCES worthy of THOTH who gave us HIS BOOK.

I need only add that it is worth noting that the Paths below Tiphereth are those of the UNITS in the Hebrew Alphabet, as this is THE FIRST ORDER. Those below the Supernal Triad are the TENS corresponding to THE SECOND ORDER while the FOUR SUPERNAL PATHS are the HUNDREDS and their NUMERATION is ONE THOUSAND which is a Large ALEPH. Thus we have THE THIRD ORDER of the HOLY QABALAH.

Section II

Those who are interested in the gradual working out and fulfillment of the Prophesies of "LIBER LEGIS"—the Book of the Law for the New Aeon—given to the world by THE MASTER THERION as a result of the EQUINOX OF THE GODS March 21st, 1904 E.V.—may note the following verses which may have a bearing on the matter just disclosed.

The Divinatory verses delivered by Therion as representing the present six-months, An XVIII Sun's passage from Aries to Libra (or March 21st, 1922 E.V. to September 21st, 1922 E.V.) are from Chapter III, Verses 70 and 71. I will quote the previous and following verses in addition.

69. There is success.

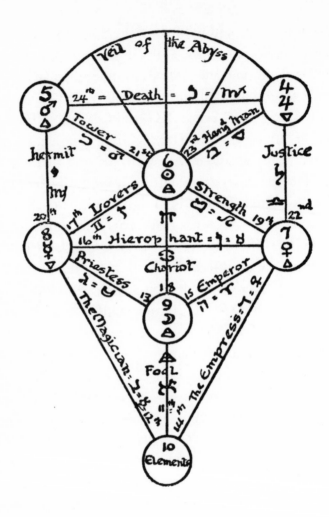

Fig. 11
(For color attributions see plate 3 between
pages 110 and 111)

70. I am the Hawk-Headed Lord of Silence and of Strength; my nemyss shrouds the night-blue sky.

71. Hail! ye twin warriors about the pillars of the world for your time is nigh at hand.

72. I am of the Lord of the Double Wand of Power; the wand of the Force of Coph Nia—but my left hand is empty, for I have crushed an Universe; and nought remains.

Without making comment on these verses I will quote one or two others which seem significant.

Ch. I. Verse 49. Abrogate are all rituals, all ordeals, all words and signs. Ra-Hoor-Khuit hath taken his seat in the East at the Equinox of the Gods; ★ ★ ★

Verse 50. There is a word to say about the Hierophantic task. Behold! there are three ordeals in one, and it may be given in three ways. The gross must pass through fire; (Note by Fra A. 𒀭 the old 31st Path.) let the fine be tried in intellect, and the lofty chosen ones in the highest; Thus ye have star & star, system & system; let not one know well the other.

(Note: FIFTY was the WORD of the last six-months).

Verse 52. If this be not aright; if ye confound the space-marks (Note. Paths between the Sephiroth?) saying: They are one; or saying, They are many, if the ritual be not ever unto me: then expect the direful judgments of Ra Hoor Khuit!

Verse 54. Change not so much as the style of a letter; for behold! thou o prophet, shall not behold all these mysteries hidden therein.

Verse 55. The child of thy bowels, *he* shall behold them.

Verse 56. ★ ★ ★ solve the first half of the equation, leave the second unattacked. But thou hast all in the clear light, and some, though not all in the dark.

(Note: One meaning of this equation may be that the Sephiroth = the Paths. The Clear Light of the Lightning Flash, and the Paths but partially interpreted.)

Verse 57 is significant; the first part should he studied with care by those in possession of Liber Legis. I quote the latter part.

"All these old letters of my Book are aright; but ש is not the Star. This also is secret: my prophet shall reveal it to the wise.

(He did, transposing The Emperor and the Star, thus bringing The Emperor to its present position. A.)

One should further note Ch. I, Verse 34, in which Nuit says: "the ordeals I write not: the rituals shall be **half known** and **half concealed**: the Law is for all."

Section III

June 2nd 1922 E.V. 6 30 P. M. (5.30 Sun time)

Since writing the above, other matters are becoming clear to me. As usual, The Book of the Law supplies the Key.

I remembered the verse from Chapter II wherein Hadit says "Come! all ye, and learn the secret that hath not yet been revealed. I, Hadit, am the complement of Nu, my bride," and I decided to look up the quotation and perhaps place it at the beginning of my Book "The Bride's Reception" for which it seemed suitable. I also intended to place at the beginning the words of Nuit, recently quoted "The gross must pass through fire; let the fine be tried in intellect, and the lofty chosen ones in the highest" thus giving a sort of hint at the secret of the Inner Order, and instituting a test of intelligence by some subtle means in the body of the book, which might lead others to make the same discovery without having read this appendix.

I had also obtained some light on Hadit's statement, for he being the SERPENT, might indicate the PATHS, while NUIT might in a measure represent THE SEPHIROTH, His complement, with possibly an additional Sephira to make ELEVEN, which is her Number.

On looking at Liber Legis I first noticed the words in Ch. I, Verse 16 wherein Hadit states "I am the Empress & the Hierophant. Thus eleven as my bride is eleven" and the mystery of the new Path of Hé, immediately presented itself to my mind once more. Then in Verse 15, just above, "The Empress and the King are not of me; for there is a further secret." The Empress and King (or Emperor) are together in my present arrangement, but the Emperor seems wrong. What this further secret is, I have not yet tried to discover, as it involves the main question of making changes in the Paths, etc.

The next words that drew my attention were in Chapter II, Verse 2, (following those I first quoted). "I am not extended, and Khabs is the name of my House." I had of course attempted various interpretations of these words before, such as "not-extended" being the extension of NOT in a mystical way concerning LA which is Not. I had also stated that I believed Malkuth to be the House of Hadit (See Liber AVM), a Closed Sphere, etc. I had remarked too, that the sum of the numbers from 1 to 31 = 496, a Perfect Number which reduces to 13 (AChD= Unity) and the Numeration of Malkuth (מלכות), but I had never put these facts together so as to read "I am NOT (LA=31) extended (1+2+3 ...+31=496) and Khabs is the name of my House," therefore MALKUTH, The Kingdom, which I fancy contains all the sephiroth. This Number (496) is also that of לויתן Leviathan, the Dragon or Serpent, which probably represents Hadit. Now it is written "The Perfect and the Perfect are one perfect and not two, nay are none."[1] This is a Perfect Number and Nuit is THE BRIDE (Malkuth = The Bride) of Hadit, may it not be that Hadit and Nuit are united in Malkuth, and that in some way this is the Eleventh Sephira (if we put in Daäth), and that "The Fool" was numbered Zero so as not to upset the THIRTY-TWO PATHS, which would otherwise be 33 viz: Two Knights on One Horse.

Section IV

June 3rd 1922 E.V.

Last night, after writing the above, I was obliged to take a Class in "The Vision and The Voice." We studied the 9th, 8th and 7th Aethyrs. During this study many illuminating ideas came to me, one I particularly remember in the 7th Aethyr (Eq. I. No. 5. Page 117) "The five and the six are balanced in the Word Abrahadabra, and therein is the mystery disclosed. But the key unto this gate (Daleth) is the balance of the seven and the four; and of this thou hast not even the first letter." I remarked to myself how clearly the Mystery of $5° = 6^\square$ is shown when THE CHARIOT is attributed to the Path from Yesod to Tiphereth, as it is in my revised Order, but also that Libra the Balance is now between Netzach and Chesed the SEVEN and the FOUR.

Also I particularly noticed the relationship of AIWASS the Minister of Ra-Hoor-Khuit, to the Seer, and to ADONAI his Lord, who is again but the Viceroy of the Unknown King. (P. 114.)

Further I was struck by the words (Page 110) of the Angel of the Pyramid, "The light is come to the darkness, and the darkness is made light. Then is light married with light & the child of their love is that other darkness, wherein they abide that have lost name and form. Therefore did I kindle him that had NOT UNDERSTANDING, and in the Book of the Law did I write the secrets of truth that are like unto a STAR and a SNAKE and a SWORD.

And unto him that UNDERSTANDETH AT LAST do I deliver the secrets of truth in such wise that the LEAST OF THE LITTLE CHILDREN OF THE LIGHT may run to the knees of the MOTHER and be brought to UNDER-STAND."

Many more points might be studied but I have not had the time. Particularly did I miss a point (noticed by Brother S. who asked me to repeat it, but I could not find the place) and it was (Page 104) "Until the Ibis be revealed unto the Crab, and the Sixfold Star become the Radiant Triangle" but this I have since been led to discover.

After arriving home at night, I picked out from the book-case THE SEPHER YETZIRAH (Dr. Westcott's translation, limited to 100 copies, published by Robt. H. Fryar, Bath 1887) and noticed some interesting passages, as follows: "Ten are the numbers of the ineffable Sephiroth, ten and not nine, ten and not eleven." (Possibly warning me from the track I was following earlier in the evening.) "Learn this wisdom, and

be wise in the understanding of it, investigate these numbers, and draw knowledge from them, FIX THE DESIGN
IN ITS PURITY, and pass from it to its Creator seated on
his throne."To this was appended the following notes:

Rittangelius gives "REPLACE THE FORMATIVE
POWER UPON HIS THRONE" Postellus gives
"RESTORE THE DEVICE OR WORKMANSHIP TO
ITS PLACE."

The above are remarkable as proof that the restoration
of the ORDER of the QABALAH is the main work. Also
it may be that having attained in ASSIAH one goes on to
the YETZIRATIC World and re-adjusts the SYMBOLS of
FORMATION. I noticed, too, some of the remarks about the
"Three Mother Letters," but could not quite see the points
indicated.

This morning I took the "Sepher Yetzirah" with me, and
on my way to the office, opened it at the following words:

"He created this universe by the three Sepharim,
Number, **Writing**, and **Speech**."This gave me food for
thought about the Three Mothers again. Then I turned idly
to the middle of the book—which contains other tracts,
among them "The Count of Gabalis." My eyes caught these
words:

An Oracle

"There is above the Celestial Fire, an Incorruptible Flame,
always sparkling; the Spring of Life, the Fountain of all Being,
the Original of all things! This Flame produceth all Things;
and Nothing perisheth, but what it consumes. It makes it

Self known by it Self. This Fire cannot be contained in any place: 'Tis without Body, and without Matter. It encompasses the Heavens: And there goes out from it a little Spark, which makes all the Fire of the Sun, of the Moon, and of the Stars."

And again another Oracle—"There is in God an immense Profundity of Flame. Nevertheless, the HEART should not fear to TOUCH this Adorable Fire, or to be touched by it: It will never be consumed by this so sweet Fire; whose MILD and Tranquil Heat, makes the Binding, the HARMONY, and the DURATION of the World. Nothing subsists but by this Fire, which is GOD Himself." This set me to thinking that the Path of SHIN must be the one from KETHER to TIPHERETH without any further shadow of doubt. Also is not this the 31st Path which Governs the SUN and MOON (Tiphereth and Yesod) which is the Origin-AL (=31) of all things wherein NOTHING (LA=NOT= 31) perisheth, but what it consumes. (Some of the words I have written Large to point out the Qabalistic ideas clearly.) By the time I had arrived at the office I had determined to set up a Tree of Life and to Place THE THREE MOTHER LETTERS on the MIDDLE PILLAR and on so doing, I again remembered the Words "He created this Universe by the THREE SEPHARIM, **Number**, **Writing** and **Speech**. Is not this the Work of Hermes the THRICE GREATEST, the Universal Mercury, and do not the Three Mother Letters thus arranged form the Caduceus; Shin above Mem above Aleph, on the Rod of the Middle Pillar, with The Winged Globe of Kether Chokmah and Binah above? Having therefore FIXED OUR MERCURY the next thing is to use

WISDOM in the WISE UNDERSTANDING of the matter so as to FIX THE DESIGN IN ITS PURITY. This I decided to do by means of the Planetary and Zodiacal Symbols only, leaving the Elements FIXED in their proper place and not worrying with the Letters or the Trumps for the moment. I first placed the Symbols in the 10 Sephiroth. Then I noticed the connection.

ש =Number=Fire.

מ =Writing which flows like Water.

א =Speech which cometh from Air.

But also ש is all these being SPIRIT so that its three flames are Water, Air, Fire indicating Binah the Root of Water, Kether the Root of Air, the Divine Breath, and Chokmah the Root of Fire—these form the Winged Globe of the Third Order. Also the Tarot Trump "The Judgment" shows this, for we have the Air coming from the Trumpet, (The Music of the Spheres), the Figures arising in the form of Fire, and the Water in the background indicating the Waters of Death, the Path of Scorpio, which is the veil of the Abyss. Also notice that this Path of Shin is divided by the reciprocal paths into THREE, as is the Path of Mem into TWO while the Path of Aleph is SINGLE and alone.

To continue, after this digression, with the Paths of the Planets and Signs. As before Mercury joins Malkuth and Hod, The Moon joins Yesod and Hod. Venus joins Malkuth and Netzach. Now we need something Ruled by VENUS, in place of the Aries attribution, this is evidently CANCER since his Path has been given to MEM. Taurus, Ruled by

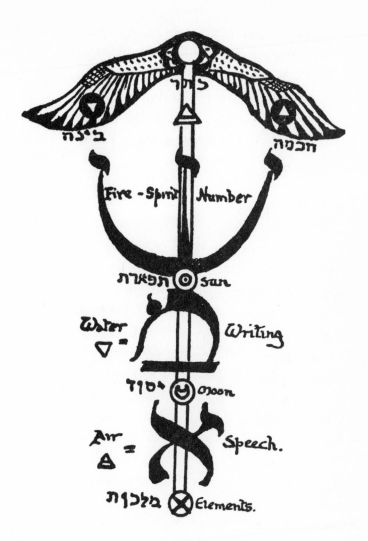

Fig. 12

Venus, unites Hod and Netzach. Gemini unites Hod and Tiphereth. Cancer has been disposed of. Leo unites Netzach and Tiphereth. Virgo unites Hod and Geburah. Libra unites Netzach and Chesed. Scorpio undoubtedly unites Geburah and Chesed. So far, up to the Veil of the Abyss, we have only two Paths unfilled. What about ARIES, Ruled by Mars, in which sign is the SUN at the VERNAL EQUINOX. This must join TIPHERETH and GEBURAH, where we had previously placed the Mars symbol. The other Path, from Tiphereth to Chesed, is not clear for the moment, so we proceed to put our certainties in order. Saggitarius, ruled by Jupiter, is tempting, but had better be reserved. Capricorn ruled by Saturn must either join Geburah to Binah, or Tiphereth to Binah, as before. The latter is undoubtedly correct for it shows "The Devil" connecting with the Sun, and AYIN uniting with NUN (Scorpio) forming ON = The Sun. This leaves but one path for the MARS Symbol, which must join Geburah and Binah. Now we must deal with AQUARIUS ruled by Saturn. There are but two vacant Paths, one from Binah to Kether and the other from Binah to Chokmah. The Tarot seems to decide this. The Woman with the STARS above her head and the WATER at her feet evidently connects the Sphere of the STARS = Chokmah with the GREAT SEA = Binah. This leaves the SATURN Symbol for the Path from Binah to Kether. Now we come to PISCES ruled by Jupiter. What could be better than using our blank path from Tiphereth to Chesed, since we have used the one on the other side for ARIES, and PISCES, the last sign, might as well meet the Sun and represent the GRAND CYCLE of the ZODIAC, with the Sun

Passing From Aries to Pisces, (as it is now passing into AQUARIUS, the old path from which we took Aries). Also The Tarot card "The Moon" shows KEPHRA Rising from the Pool and this Symbol again indicates the conjunction of Sun and Moon, which was Symbolized in the SECOND ORDER in a secret manner. This, combined with the fact that Pisces is Ruled by Jupiter, completes the evidence, in favour of our choice. We have now but three Symbols left, the SUN, JUPITER and SAGITTARIUS and we have Three Paths—from Kether to Chokmah, from Chokmah to Chesed and from Chokmah to Tiphereth. If the SUN is to unite with Tiphereth, there is only one Path for it, that from Chokmah to Tiphereth. We still have JUPITER to arrange for, as well as SAGITTARIUS ruled by JUPITER. Obviously, since there is only one Path out of Chesed, we cannot give it to Two Symbols. I prefer to give it to Jupiter, though one of the Symbols has to be placed among the SUPERNALS and it might be this one. Anyway, leave Him there for the Present while we attempt to decide the important question of SOL and SAGITTARIUS. Can Sagittarius be the Path from Kether to Chokmah? It does not seem likely, but it might be the ARROW across the ABYSS from Tiphereth to Chokmah, as it were Tiphereth's connection with the Star Universe.

The Tarot Card "Temperance" (= Sagittarius) shows a figure who is pouring fluid from one vessel to another, and in the old cards one vessel is Red and the other Blue. Can this indicate the Red of the Path of Shin and the Blue of Chesed? This card should be Ruled by Jupiter, and this would indicate the connection, especially if we remember that the Waters of Death and the Waters of Life may contain an occult

Mystery, and this path crosses Nun, or Scorpio. There can be little doubt of this attribution. This really leaves the disputed Supernal Path (from Kether to Chokmah), either to The SUN or JUPITER, and I had in my design this morning given it to the SUN, which makes the attributions wonderfully perfect. I now once more intend to change the arrangement, though tentatively, leaving this the final question to the Higher Powers. With Jupiter, The Father of The Gods, joining Kether and Chokmah, we should find THE WHEEL OF FORTUNE (representing the PRIMUM MOBILE or the BEGINNING of the WHIRLING MOTIONS, also the THREE PRINCIPLES and the CENTRUM IN CENTRI TRIGONO) producing the System of Revolving Orbs in CHOKMAH. Also in the "Heavenly Hexagram" Kether is attributed to Jupiter. In that case the SUN will be the Path from CHOKMAH to TIPHERETH (and this represents Him as taking up his work as THE LOGOS of the SOLAR SYSTEM) and the Path from CHESED to CHOKMAH will be SAGITTARIUS which is naturally Ruled by Jupiter. This Makes all the Signs of the Zodiac meet their Rulers perfectly. Also the 32nd Path is called the "Administrative Intelligence," and this is the office of Jupiter, although of course The Sun may be said to Rule the Planets. Anyway the Holy Spirit of the 31st Path governs the Sun and Moon without doubt and is Ruler under Kether of the Central Pillar.

Now I have only a few more remarks to make in order to complete my day's investigations. NUIT says "Change not so much as the style of a letter," and again "All these old letters of my book are aright, but ‭ℸ‬ is not the Star." I think this means that 𐤀 is NOT (= LA = 31) the Star, for She is combined with the Origin-AL Shin (Hadit) of the 31st Path, and is Herself the 29th Path which =11. This was the 4th path of the Old System and 31=3+1=4. I shall therefore leave all the attributions of Letters and Cards as they were, all that one has to do is to arrange them in their proper order, and BEHOLD. This is the Mystery of the THIRD ORDER of the QABALAH, it being the THIRD ORDER of the PATHS and it is for those who are to be tried in the HIGHEST viz: (the decision between the SUN and JUPITER). THE FIRST ORDER is for those who must PASS THROUGH FIRE, the SECOND ORDER is to try the INTELLECT, and THE THIRD ORDER for those who have COORDINATED their UNDERSTANDING.

Just a few more notes made this morning. HADIT says: "I am the EMPRESS and the HIEROPHANT, thus eleven, as my bride is eleven." Considering our new Plan we find the Hierophant, Taurus, on the Path from HOD to NETZACH and THE EMPRESS joining MALKUTH to NETZACH, while between them is CANCER on the Path attributed to the EMPEROR or KING in the SECOND ORDER. But CHETH (= 418) should be the HIEROPHANT in the NEW AEON and therefore take the place of the Past Hierophant, OSIRIS, THE BULL. The Hierophant, in a certain sense, passes to the Path of Cancer and THE CHARIOT to the Path of TAURUS, without changing the marking of the cards in any way. Then we find the OLD HIEROPHANT taking the Place of the EMPEROR, or Hé, and the Hierophant, being Vau, unites the Son and Daughter, since CHETH ח the path of the

THIRD ORDER is a letter like ה (Hé), but CONNECTED at the UPPER LINE or HEAD, so that the letter is really like THE HEAD = ר = The Sun connected with ו the Son. These letters produce RV the Root of AIR (= the FOOL), also of ROTA the WHEEL. Also note that Cancer the CRAB goeth sideways, which is the move of the HIEROPHANT, or BISHOP, in CHESS. Thus also has the Past Hierophant gone sideways, for the old Aeon is passed away and all things are Ruled by the one in the CHARIOT who hath harnessed the BLACK AND WHITE SPHINXES and sits on the CUBIC STONE which is (YESOD) THE FOUNDATION of the UNIVERSE. HOOR in his secret name and splendour is the LORD INITIATING and HIS CHARIOT rolls STRAIGHT AHEAD.

Aumn
Section V

June 3rd 11.49 P. M. (Sun time 10.49)
Liber Legis. Ch. I. Verse 49.

"Abrogate are all rituals, all ordeals, all words and signs. Ra-Hoor-Khuit hath taken his seat in the East at the Equinox of the Gods; and let Asar be with Isa, who also are one. But they are not of me. Let Asar be the adorant, Isa, the sufferer; Hoor in his secret **name** and **splendour** is the Lord initiating."

Note: ASAR = The Bull = Taurus, let him be, (that is remain) with ISA (The Hanged Man, = Mem), who also are one, viz: their Paths cross on the Tree of Life (Third Order).

HOOR in his secret NAME and SPLENDOUR is the Lord initiating, viz: Hoor is to be considered as on the Path from Hod=SPLENDOUR to Netzach, thus indicating him as the Victorious One, though his attributions to Cancer and the Path from Yesod to Netzach must remain the same. But there is much more than this, for ה (Hé) became the Path of ו (Vau) when the Bull symbolically passed to the place of the Past Hierophant, viz: the Path of ח (Cheth) thus וה (Vau-Hé) were united, even as it is clear that The Daughter = "The World" = ת (Tau) has also been raised to the THRONE of the MOTHER, for ת is now on the Path from Binah to Kether, where she was first tempted by the old Serpent, Saturn. Thus we obtain the idea HV, but we also found CHETH, the New Hierophant or Lord Initiating = ו, combined with ר, which is VR. Now then, these ideas combine into HVVR which is HOOR, or we can say that ה (Hé) is Resh and Vau separated, and obtain HRU or HERU. Also if the Vau be reversed and added to Resh, or rather combined with it, we get ת (Tau) = VT the letters shown on the old Tarot trump the Chariot. But we must not actually change the Unity of the arrangement as it stands, for we find the Triad Malkuth, Yesod, Netzach, joined by the Paths Aleph, Cheth, Daleth, which is Achad=Unity (and Ahebah, Love through 13) which is the mystery of the Uniting of the Son and Daughter.

Now HOOR spelt הוור = 217 = 10, Malkuth or Kether or IO = Jove, etc., (see Mystery of Jupiter in the Supernal Triad). But spelt העער = 345 and this suggests the 47th problem of Euclid and Masonry. Now the Sephiroth 3-4-5 suggest these proportions on the Tree, then the "lost path" across the Abyss would be shown in this triangle. What do we obtain?

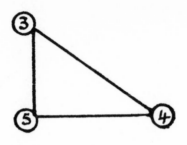

Fig. 13

The Egyptian ISIS, OSIRIS, HORUS. Not that alone, however, but the Magic SQUARES of SATURN, JUPITER and MARS. Now note, the Supernal Paths are Saturn and Jupiter, did these two MALES give birth to the Idea of MARS, and thus, as we see indicated by the Mars square in diagram which covers the old path of Aleph, produce the Bastard of the Swastika (For the Swastika is 17 on the Square of Mars) thus causing the confusion of ideas in regard to the Old Path of Aleph, as representing the first creative Path, when this should have been the path of Shin, the Holy Spirit and the Universal Mercury. Herein is perhaps the Mystery of the THREE LOST FATHERS, Saturn, Jupiter and Mars (or Horus the Elder) for they all got lost somewhere and are represented by the THREE MOTHERS, forming the Caduceus of the Universal Mercury, which represents both Male and Female in one.

Again referring to Cancer ♋ = 69 by shape = Sameck the Prop and Teth the Serpent. Not bad for the Serpent and Staff of Moses, and it may be that The Arrow or Prop will yet be

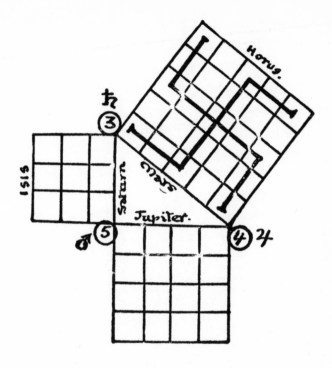

Fig. 14

the means of raising the Serpent to its true estate. 217 (HVVR) also equals the Hebrew word for AIR which is Aleph = 1 and these ideas combined give 69+1 = 70 = The Eye. But the new Hierophant CHETH = 418, and 418 is the Numeration of HRU-RA-HA which is the WORD of this present Equinox (Sun in Aries). HERU, we have already explained. Ra may be THE SUN, or AR (Ch) LIGHT (of which 5=6 or ABRAHADABRA = 418 is the KEY in the SECOND ORDER) then HA is perhaps Hé or some Mystery of the Third Order. I suggest that it has to do with

ALEPH, whose change of POSITION was the KEY of the SECOND ORDER, and Hé which had to be changed and whose path was taken by CHETH (= 418) in the Third Order. The present arrangement of the paths gives A, Ch, D if read in one direction but D, A, Ch = 4, 1, 8, if we continue the cycle. Anyway the Initials of Heru-Ra-Ha = HRH = 210 which is a very significant number in the New Aeon.

Now note the 74th verse of Ch. III of Liber Legis. "There is a splendour in my name hidden and glorious, as the Sun of midnight is ever the Son." Does not this again suggest the SPLENDOUR and NAME of the Victorious One.

Again, in the next and last verse of the book. "The ending of the words is the Word Abrahadabra" (= 418 = PARZIVAL = The FOOL. See Ch. I "And Ahrahadabra. It shall be his child and that strangely.") The Book of the Law is Written and concealed. Aum (= 111= Aleph the Fool) Ha.(= 6 =Vau = The Son and the Lord Initiating who is now CHETH=418.)

Finally note 345 = Shin, Mem, and Hé. The last letter is the Breath of the Holy Spirit or Air, thus suggesting the arrangement of the Three Mothers in their true position.

Section VI

Sun. June 4th.

Last night further Mysteries began to clear up in a wonderful manner. The Supernal Triad is now composed of the Three Sephiroth joined by the Paths of JUPITER, SATURN and AQUARIUS or The WHEEL, The UNIVERSE and The STAR. But it is written (although I explained this in another manner formerly) "TZADDI is NOT the STAR,"[2]

But we had THREE paths that were difficult to adjust, all of which had a claim. One of these was RESH the SUN. Suppose we substitute this for TZADDI, what should we see? THE THREE PATHS joining the SUPERNAL TRIAD would then be KAPH, TAU, RESH=KThR= KETHER the CROWN. But if Tzaddi is Not the Star then perhaps RESH is THE STAR as well as the LETTER of THE SUN. This would show the whole Mystery of the UNIVERSE, the WHEEL, the SUN, STARS, PLANETS and ELEMENTS, all in the SUPERNAL TRIAD, which is the STAR of the THIRD ORDER, the Three-fold Star. And look at the NUMBERS of the SEPHIROTH COMBINED, for the first Mystery of the SEPHARIM is NUMBER. 1+2=3 The TRINITY. 1+3=4 The Tetrad. 2+3=5 The Flaming Star. 1 and 2 combined = 12 = הוא =HUA (ה referred to Mater ו to Pater and א to Corona), etc. 13—Achad, Unity and AHBH Love, etc. 23 = Joy and Life. 21 = אהיה = Existence, Being, the KETHER name of God. 31 = אל = God and All, לא = Not. 31 is also the Key of the Book of the Law, etc. 32 = אהיהוה the 32-fold name in which AHIH and IHVH are coalesced which, if the three Hé's are taken for THE THREE MOTHERS, gives 358 = The Messiah and also the Serpent. There are many other important attributions. Thus all cometh from KThR the Crown, which containeth the Mystery of the three Fathers Jupiter, Saturn and Sol, and the Three Whirling forces of Life in The WHEEL, the SWASTIKA FIGURE in The STAR, and The ELLIPSE of The UNIVERSE.

There are other Mysteries about these alternative Paths, which may mean something, although they do not conflict with this truly wonderful Trinity in Unity. For had the

ARROW=Sagittarius (Ruled by Jupiter) been put in the place of Jupiter, and the Spirit, SHIN, been included in the CENTRE of the TRIAD we should have obtained the Numeration 60+400+200+300=960 which plus the 3 Sephiroth = 963 = אחד = ACHAD = UNITY (Spelt fully) also the Hebrew for Garland, Crown, a little wreath. May not this be the Crown of Victory on the head of 418 (as Cheth) in the midst of אד the "Mist and Vapour" which concealed him in UNITY, which is ALEPH, which is THE PURE FOOL.

Section VII

June 5th 1922

NOTES

Possible date of Plan of Qabalah indicated by SUN between ARIES and PISCES in Grand Cycle of Zodiac.

Note. Change in position of ה places this path in connection with SUN=Son. Marriage of Daughter to Son.

Note. SWORD, SNAKE and STAR. Three Orders.

Note. Lion = Leo, lies down with Lamb=Aries.

Note. Horoscope for 31st, Mercury entering Cancer, is very remarkable and seems to indicate Aeon of MAAT.

Note. SUN of MIDNIGHT may indicate Resh attributed to STAR.

Note. KEYS of SUPERNALS XXI and X=31 also Path 1–2 = Three Principles on Wheel. 1–3 = Four Elements in World 2–3 = Flaming Star or Sun and Star combined. 1–6 = 31st Path. etc.

Section VIII

June 5th Midnight (Sun time)

I have been making further considerations in the Light of a Colour Plan of the Third Order which I made to-day (see plate 4 between pages 110 and 111).

I perceive, (1) that the Paths of Gemini and Virgo should be interchanged in order to make the harmony more perfect (2) I began further investigation of the Supernal Triad according to the NUMBERS of the KEYS. I find that the Symbolism is indeed perfect if we substitute the actual Sun card for Aquarius, thus we obtain:

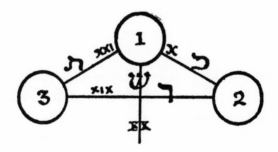

Fig. 15

KThR = Kether The Crown (as before from LETTERS.) XXI+X = 31.

XXI+X+XIX = 50, and it is written: "FIFTY are Gates of UNDERSTANDING," while SHIN, the Path from 1-6, = XX which plus 50 = 70 = AYIN = THE EYE (in the TRI-ANGLE). Now Tzaddi is not the Star for the Star is THE EYE = Ayin. Therefore Ayin is the Star and Tzaddi the Devil.

Now 70, The Eye, plus the SPIRIT = 300 = 370 is
A'ASH = CREATION. The STAR should now be the Path
from CHOKMAH to TIPHERETH thus Harmonizing the
Sun and Zodiac. The Path of NUN, which intersects those
of Ayin and Tzaddi, gives us N.O.X. = Night and the SHIN
=The Light that shineth in darkness and the Darkness comprehendeth it not." Also the Swastika represents 4 L's = 30 x
4 =120, that is 4-fold Justice, and ON the Key of the City of
Babalon. Again ע & נ ON, are united since the Paths join.
Also עצ = The Tree (of Life) and also suggests OX = א. Now
note "Twenty-two are the Mansions of My Father, but there
cometh an OX that shall set his forehead against the house
and it shall fall, for all these things are the toys of the Magician
and the Maker of Illusions, that barreth the Understanding
from the Crown" (See Vision and Voice Page 142).

Note also how "Love is the law, love under will" is clearly
shown on the Tree, for Love (Venus) is the Law (Libra) love
(Chesed) under (Sameck = Temperance) Will (Chokmah).

I notice also that this should be the emphasized statement for "Love IS the law" and "The Law IS for ALL." While
"Do what thou wilt SHALL BE the whole of the Law,"
implies, in one way, the future, for this freedom must be won.

Note "Thou hast made MAN a little lower than the
Elohim, (86), Thou hast Crowned him with Glory and
Honour. The Paths of 666 now unite with Tiphereth and
Hod, but 86 is AHIH ADNI.

Section IX
Of the Mysteries of the Beginning

בראשית

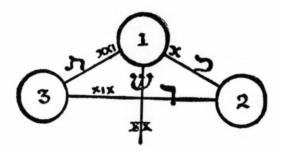

Fig. 16

June 8th, 1922. Last night further mysteries were opened up to me. Firstly כ, (Kaph)= 20 conceals the letter י (IVD), for this letter, spelt in full = 20. Again יוד (IVD) is concealed in the shape of the letter א (Aleph). Therefore when it was written (Gen. I. 1) "In the Beginning," this meaning "In the Head" or "In Wisdom," the word ראשית (RASHITH, The Head) suggests ר (Resh) which is one of the Paths of the Supernal Triad, just as the Path of כ (KAPH) The Palm of the Hand, suggests י (Yod) The Hand, as well as concealing it numerically as shown above. But the word ראשית is all to be found in KThR, The Supernal Triad of the Crown, for the first letter Resh is the Path from Chokmah to Binah, Aleph can be traced through Kaph as above shown, Shin is the Holy Spirit in the midst, Yod is concealed in Kaph, and Tau is the Path from Kether to Binah. But the word used in Genesis is בראשית (B'RAShITh) which is "IN THE

Beginning," but since ר (Resh) comes on the Reciprocal Path, or Horizontal line, we see that ר with this line as the base, forms כ. Thus the whole word may be traced to the Supernal Triad.

Again, כ (Kaph) is the Trump numbered X = Yod by numeration and Aleph, by shape. And as the Trumps XXI+X = 31 = אל the WORD of Kether, so also כ, since it conceals י represents פ (Pé), The MOUTH which utters the WORD of WISDOM or CHOKMAH.

It is interesting to note the symbolism of the letters of the Supernal Paths when spelt in full. Resh = ריש, and we see this also conceals the Yod or tongue and the Holy Triple Spirit SHIN, and these Paths of Resh and Shin are conjoined. Again SHIN (שין) conceals the Yod, (as it does THE THREE MOTHERS) and it terminates in NUN, which Path it crosses before it enters TIPHERETH = THE SUN, which was RESH in the Supernal Triad. And TAU = תו = TV and this conceals the VAU or Son as well as by SHAPE ר and ו, RU=The Divine Breath, or Ruach Elohim. This again is the Root of Rota the Wheel, which is shown in the Path of Kaph the Wheel of Fortune. But in Tau = "The Universe" we see the Ellipse, therefore is it suggested that The Whirling of the Primum Mobile (Rashith ha Galgalim) was first about an axis, and then the Whole revolution took an elliptic Path. Notice also how ש = 300 = Ruach Elohim, and again, that the Path of Shin, 300 united with Kether = 1 = 301 = ASH = Fire, while this number 301 is equal to "My Lord the Faithful King" who liveth and reigneth for ever and ever. Again Kaph conceals Aleph and Pé, The Air

and the Mouth, since in full it is כאף = KAP. Also it is written that God made a covenant with Abraham concerning
the Number Ten (The Sephiroth, etc.) and that this refers to
The Ten fingers of the Hands and the Ten toes of the feet
and also to the Covenant of the Tongue and of Circumcision.
Now Yod is the Phallus, and Tau is the Phallus in extension,
and Resh is the Head of the Phallus, (with its concealed Eye)
and Kaph is the Palm of the Hand which conceals the Yod,
and as shown, the Yod and the Kaph = Pé, The Mouth which
uttered the Covenant, and Aleph is His Holy Covenant. (See
Vision and Voice and Sepher Yetzirah in regard to these statements.) And Resh, the Head, combined with the line forms
BETH which is the House of God, in which SHIN, the
HOLY SPIRIT is concealed. Also BETH is MERCURY,
but this is THE UNIVERSAL MERCURY which conceals
the THREE MOTHERS, which form the CENTRAL
PILLAR OF THE TREE by which "One Ran and
Returned," as also, HE COMBINES in HIS SYMBOL, ALL
THE PLANETS including the SUN and MOON. For HE
represents the SUPREME INTELLIGENCE of the
BEGINNING.

A few further considerations. The Sephiroth Kether,
Tiphereth, Yesod and Malkuth = 1+ 6+9+ 10 = 26 = יהוה.
Binah, Geburah and Hod = 3, 5, 8 = 358 The Serpent and
the Messiah. And Netzach, Chesed and Chokmah = 7, 4, 2
= 742 = The Ark of the Covenant.

Also Binah, Chokmah and Tiphereth = 3, 2, 6 and 326
is יהשוה = JEHESUAH, or the Descent of the Holy Spirit,
ש Into the Four Elements יהוה the Old Jehovah.

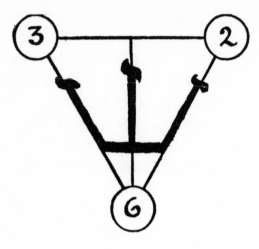

Fig. 17

And the numbers of the Sephiroth— Binah + Geburah + Hod + Malkuth + Netzach + Chesed and Chokmah = 3+5+8+10+7+4+2 = 39 = the Eternal One, and together with those of the Middle Pillar 1+6+9+10 = 26 we obtain 39+26 = 65 = ADONAI.—The Lord.

Section X

Enough has been written in regard to THESE HOLY MYS-TERIES, which are Mysteries no longer in the old sense of the word. Enough, at least, to prove without shadow of doubt the fulfillment of some of the prophesies of both the Old and New Books of the Law, to make possible the Plans for a Perfect Temple and a true Understanding of the Holy Covenant. This Universal Temple is lit by the Holy Spirit of the One True God, so that in very truth, (as it was written by the Prophet of the New Aeon, 666 the Beast, in the "Vision and the Voice" in the 8th Aethyr). "To him that UNDER-STANDETH AT LAST do I deliver the secrets of truth in such wise that the least of the little children of the light may run to the knees of the great mother and be brought to Understand." For this Great Mother is MAAT the Lady of TRUTH of whom it is prophesied in Liber Legis in a veiled manner Chapter 3, verse 34. (see comment Eqx. Vol. 1. 7) and also more openly in Liber A'ASH (=Creation) Equinox Vol. I, 6: "Set is his holy covenant which he shall display in the great day of M. A. A. T. that is, being interpreted the Master of the Temple of A∴A∴ whose name is Truth." For yet again notice that the Key Letter of the Change from the First to the Second Order is Aleph, and the changed letters in the Third Order are Hé, Resh, Vau, Mem, Cheth, Yod, Sameck, so that in all we have the one Secret Name

HRUMACHIS,

which is Three Hundred and Thirty, that is to say, THE HOLY SPIRIT of TRUTH and JUSTICE.

Finis.

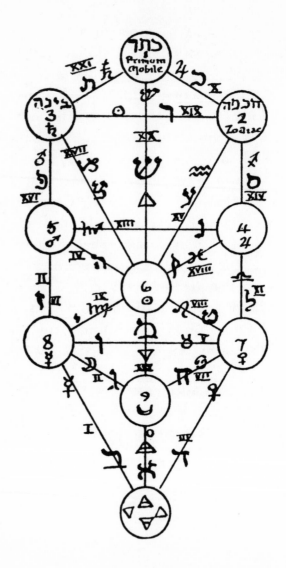

Key to plate 4 (between pages 110 and 111)

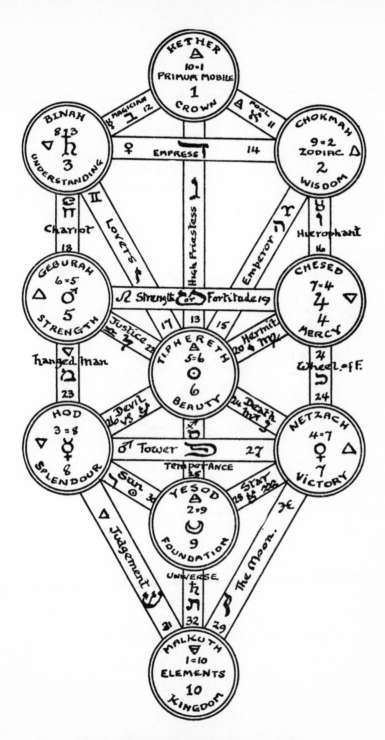

Tree of Life with Correspondences.

NOTES

Note not denoted by *"Editor's Note"* are
Jones' footnotes from 1st edition.

Introduction to the 2005 Edition

1. Aleister Crowley, "John St. John," pp. 10–11, in *The Equinox* I(1) (1909). Reprinted York Beach, ME: Weiser Books, 1998.
2. From *The Starry Wisdom* by Lon Milo DuQuette, preface to *Polaria*, by W. H. Müller (Albuquerque, NM: Brotherhood of Life Publishing, 1996), p. 7.
3. Jones was born in London in 1886 and died in Vancouver 1950. "Achad," אחד, is Hebrew for "One" and "Unity."
4. The initiatory Grade structure of the A∴A∴ represents progressively higher states of consciousness and is symbolized as a climb up the ten Sephiroth (emanations) of the Qabalistic diagram known as the Tree of Life. The lowest ($1° = 10^\square$) is the lowest (Neophyte). The $1°$ indicates it is the first degree of the system, and the $10^\square$ indicates that the degree represents the

level of consciousness embodied in the 10th Sephira, Malkuth.

5. Jeanne Robert Foster (*neé* Olivier, 1884–1970); her magical motto was Soror Hilarion.

6. Aleister Crowley, *The Confessions of Aleister Crowley* ed. John Symonds and Kenneth Grant (Reprinted London and New York: Arkana, 1989), p. 801.

7. op. cit., p. 807.

8. Received by Aleister Crowley in 1904 e.v., *Liber AL vel Legis, The Book of the Law*, is the primary Holy Book of Thelema. It is found in numerous texts including *Liber ABA, Book Four*, 2d ed., ed. Hymenaeus Beta (York Beach, ME: Weiser Books, 1997). pp. 303–386.

9. Charles Stansfeld Jones, *Liber 31*, ed. T. Allen Greenfield (Marietta, GA: Luxor Press, 1998).

10. op. cit., p. 2.

11. *Liber AL vel Legis, The Book of the Law*, I: 76.

12. *Liber AL vel Legis, The Book of the Law*, III: 47.

13. We must not dismiss the possibility that, from our "below the abyss" point of view, these two ideas might be in essence the same thing.

14. See page 47 of this edition.

15. Aleister Crowley, et al. *The Vision and the Voice: with Commentary and Other Papers* (York Beach, ME: Weiser Books, 1998), p. 226. "One" in Hebrew is "Achad," and "Eno" is the brand name of an English laxative.

16. Stephen Skinner, ed., *The Magical Diaries of Aleister Crowley* (York Beach, ME: Weiser Books, 1996). p. 127.

17. Aleister Crowley, et al. *Magick, Liber ABA, Book Four,* 2nd rev. ed. Hymenaeus Beta (York Beach, ME: Weiser Books, 1997), p. 141.
18. Jones's letter to Gerald Yorke, April, 1948.

Introduction

1. Christian David Ginsburg (1831-1914). English Hebrew scholar, translator, and commentator.

Chapter 1

1. *Editor's Note:* Aleister Crowley, *Liber Libre, Sub Figura XXX, The Equinox* I(1) (1909), p. 17.
2. Q = XVIII = The Moon = Illusion.
   B = I = The Magician = Juggler.
   L = XI = Justice = Libra = The Balance.
3. See *The Collected Works of Aleister Crowley*, vol. II (1906, reprinted, Des Plains, IL: Yogi Publications Society, n.d.), p. 223.
4. In a certain sense Nuit and Hadit. *Editor's Note:* See Crowley's Introduction to *Liber AL vel Legis, The Book of the Law*. (London: OTO, 1938). p. 10.
5. *Editor's Note:* II Chronicles, 5:13.
6. *Editor's Note:* op. cit.
7. *Editor's Note:* S.L. MacGregor Mathers, ed. *The Kabbalah Unveiled*. (York Beach, ME: Weiser, 1997), p. 20.

Chapter 3

1. *Editor's Note*: Shin does double duty representing the quintessential 5th element, Spirit, as well as the element Fire.
2. See *Book 777*, London 1909. *Editor's Note: 777 and Other Qabalistic Writings of Aleister Crowley* (York Beach, ME: Weiser Books, Inc., 1990).

Chapter 5

1. All the true titles of the Court and small cards may be found in Equinox Vol. I, Number 8 or on "The Wheel of the Tarot" designed by Frater Achad.

Chapter 6

1. *Editor's Note*: The opening lines of the alchemical text, *The Emerald Tablet of Hermes.*
2. *Editor's Note*: From "The Oath of a Probationer" of the A∴A∴, *Liber Collegii Sancti.*

Chapter 8

1. *Editor's Note*: Frater Perdurabo (I will endure to the end), The Neophyte motto of Aleister Crowley.
2. *Editor's Note: 777 and Other Qabalistic Writings of Aleister Crowley* (1990).
3. *Editor's Note*: Habuiah, Angel of the 2 of Cups. 68th Angel of the Shemhamphorash. Rules 5°–10°. ♋.

4. *Editor's Note:* This and the following references to KDLCK refer to KABBALA DENUDATA cuius Pars Prima continet Locos Communes Kabbalisticos, Trans. S. L. MacGregor Mathers. Reprinted in abridged form 1974 as the *Kabbalah Unveiled* (York Beach, ME: Weiser Books, Inc.).

5. *Editor's Note: Siphra Dtzenioutha, The Book of Concealed Mystery,* A book of the Zohar in Knorr von Rosenroth's *Kabbalah Denudata* and abridged in Mather's *The Kabbalah Unveiled.* op. cit.

6. *Editor's Note:* Published as *The Goetia: The Lesser Key of Solomon* (Clavicula Solomonis). Ed. Aleister Crowley, trans. S.L. MacGregor Mathers (York Beach, ME: Weiser, 1995).

7. *Editor's Note:* Vehuiah, Angel of the 5 of Wands. 1st Angel of the Shemhamphorash. Rules 0°-5° Leo.

8. *Editor's Note:* Bihelami, Angel of the 1st decan of Pisces.

9. *Editor's Note:* Mekekiel, Angel of the 9 of Swords. 42nd Angel of the Shemhamphorash. Rules 15°-20° Gemini.

10. *Editor's Note:* Caliel, Angel of the 4 of Swords. 18th Angel of the Shemhamphorash. Rules 25°-30° Gemini.

11. *Editor's Note:* Aleister Crowley, *The Vision and the Voice: with Commentary and Other Papers* (York Beach, ME: Weiser Books, Inc., 1998).

Chapter 9

1. *Editor's Note*: *The Book of the Law*, (ch. I, 54) states in no uncertain terms "Change not as much as the style of a letter." Each of these three quotes from the text contains one subtle error in punctuation: there are no periods to close the first two quotes, and the third (and perhaps the most recognizable phrase of the entire book) is ended with an exclamation point instead of a period. The casual reader may dismiss these aberrations as insignificant oversights (which, indeed, they may be). Many Thelemites, however, take these matters very seriously, and given the revolutionary doctrines set forth in *Q.B.L.*, may consider the possibility that Achad may have (if only on a subconscious level) allowed these errors to go uncorrected.

2. *Editor's Note*: The Quotation is from I, 33–34 of *Liber AL vel Legis, The Book of the Law.* "Then the priest fell into a deep trance or swoon, & said unto the Queen of Heaven; Write unto us the ordeals; write unto us the rituals; write unto us the law! But she said: the ordeals I write not: the rituals shall be half known and half concealed: the Law is for all."

3. *Editor's Note*: Frater Per Ardua, Captain (later Major General) J. F. C. Fuller.

4. *Editor's Note*: Greek, "OU MH," which may be translated "Certainly Not," which was Crowley's motto in the Grade of Adeptus Exemptus.

5. *Editor's Note*: Quote is from *The Book of the Law*, I, 56.

Chapter 10

1. *Editor's Note*: Johannes Stephanus Rittangelius, professor of Hebrew in Konigsberg, who translated the Sepher Yetzirah into Latin in 1642.
2. Guillaume Barentonius Postellus (1510–1581) professor in mathematics and oriental languages at the Collège de France in 1539, translated the Sepher Yetzirah into Latin.
3. *Editor's Note*: See *The Vision and the Voice*, First Aethyr.

Appendix

1. *Editor's Note*: *The Book of the Law*, I: 45.
2. *Editor's Note*: *The Book of the Law*, I: 57.

TO OUR READERS

Weiser Books, an imprint of Red Wheel/Weiser, publishes books across the entire spectrum of occult and esoteric subjects. Our mission is to publish quality books that will make a difference in people's lives without advocating any one particular path or field of study. We value the integrity, originality, and depth of knowledge of our authors.

Our readers are our most important resource, and we appreciate your input, suggestions, and ideas about what you would like to see published. Please feel free to contact us, to request our latest book catalog, or to be added to our mailing list.

Red Wheel/Weiser, LLC
P.O. Box 612
York Beach, ME 03910-0612
www.redwheelweiser.com